REVIEWER PRAISE OF BOOKS BY DOUGLAS GRAY

Making Money in Real Estate

"Gray delivers the goods. It is all-Canadian, and not a retread book full of tips that are worthless north of the U.S. border. It's chock-full of practical streetsmart strategies and advice, pitfalls to avoid, samples, what-to-look-out for, checklists and information."
— *Business in Vancouver*

"...provides consumer insights into securing the best deal and avoiding the pitfalls...Gray's legal background has given him valuable insights."
— *The Edmonton Journal*

"Outstanding...peppered with practical no-nonsense tips...invaluable information throughout."
— *Calgary Herald*

The Complete Canadian Small Business Guide (with Diana Gray)

"This guide is truly a gold mine...an admirable job...taps into the author's expertise."
— *Profit Magazine*

"Excellent...geared especially to Canadians, unlike most small business guides."
— *Financial Times*

"The most informative and comprehensive guide on this subject matter."
— *The Toronto Star*

Home Inc.: The Canadian Home-Based Business Guide

"Should be required reading for all potential home-basers...authoritative, current and comprehensive."
— *The Edmonton Journal*

"An absolute necessity for your bookshelf...crammed with useful information."
— *Victoria Times-Colonist*

The Complete Canadian Franchise Guide (with Norm Friend)

"Down to earth, comprehensive, easy to read and packed with practical information. A superb guide to buying a franchise. Invaluable samples and checklists. Highly recommended."
— Terry and Fran Banting, Franchisees

The Canadian Snowbird Guide

"...an invaluable guide to worry-free part-time living in the U.S....by one of Canada's bestselling authors of business and personal finance books..."
— *The Globe and Mail*

"...Gray has written a reference book, thoughtful and complete, and prepared with the authoritative research skills and knowledge of a fastidious solicitor...as practical as a sunhat on a Tampa afternoon, and that alone warrants it a place on every southbound RV's bookshelf."
— *Quill & Quire*

The Canadian Guide to Will and Estate Planning (with John Budd)

"...An informative, practical guide...the authors...cover all the bases."
— *The National Post*

"...A bargain for its price, it should be part of every family's library."
— *The Globe and Mail*

Mortgages Made Easy

BESTSELLING BOOKS BY DOUGLAS GRAY

REAL ESTATE TITLES

*Making Money in Real Estate: The Canadian Guide to Profitable
Investment in Residential Property*

101 Streetsmart Condo Buying Tips for Canadians

Real Estate Investing for Canadians for Dummies
(with Peter Mitham)

Mortgages Made Easy: The All-Canadian Guide to Home Financing

*Home Buying Made Easy: The Canadian Guide to Purchasing a
Newly Built or Pre-Owned Home*

*Condo Buying Made Easy: The Canadian Guide to Apartment and
Townhouse Condos, Co-ops and Timeshares*

Mortgage Payment Tables Made Easy

SMALL BUSINESS TITLES

Start and Run a Consulting Business

Start and Run a Profitable Business Using Your Computer

*Have You Got What It Takes? The Entrepreneur's Complete Self-
Assessment Guide*

Marketing Your Product (with Donald Cyr)

The Complete Canadian Small Business Guide
(with Diana Gray)

Home Inc.: The Canadian Home-Based Business Guide
(with Diana Gray)

Raising Money: The Canadian Guide to Successful Business Financing
(with Brian Nattrass)

The Complete Canadian Franchise Guide (with Norm Friend)

So You Want to Buy a Franchise? (with Norm Friend)
Be Your Own Boss: The Ultimate Guide to Buying a Small Business or Franchise in Canada (with Norm Friend)
The Canadian Small Business Legal Guide

PERSONAL FINANCE/RETIREMENT PLANNING TITLES

The Canadian Snowbird Guide: Everything You Need to Know about Living Part-time in the U.S.A. and Mexico
The Canadian Guide to Will and Estate Planning (with John Budd)
Risk-Free Retirement: The Complete Canadian Planning Guide (with Tom Delaney, Graham Cunningham, Les Solomon and Dr. Des Dwyer)

SOFTWARE PROGRAMS

Making Money in Real Estate (jointly developed by Douglas Gray and Phoenix Accrual Corporation)

Mortgages Made Easy

The All-Canadian Guide to Home Financing

by
Douglas Gray

John Wiley & Sons Canada, Ltd.

Copyright © 2006 by Douglas Gray

Library and Archives Canada Cataloguing in Publication Data

Gray, Douglas A
   Mortgages made easy : the all-Canadian guide to home financing / Douglas A. Gray.

Includes index.
ISBN-13 978-0-470-83732-0
ISBN-10 0-470-83732-2

    I. Mortgage loans—Canada. I. Title.

HG2040.5.C2G73 2006   332.7'22'0971   C2005-906320-3

Production Credits:
Cover design: Ian Koo
Interior text design: Mike Chan
Printer: Printcrafters Inc.

John Wiley & Sons Canada, Ltd.
6045 Freemont Blvd.
Mississauga, Ontario
L5R 4J3

Printed in Canada

1 2 3 4 5 PC 10 09 08 07 06

Contents

~ CONTENTS ~

Acknowledgements

I am grateful for the kind assistance given me by many parties, including the Canada Mortgage and Housing Corporation, the Canadian Real Estate Association, Genworth Financial Canada, and Royal LePage.

I would like to thank Nicole Langlois for the superb quality of editing that she has demonstrated throughout. Her insights, creative suggestions, and positive attitude made the editorial experience a most pleasurable one.

I would like to thank the staff of John Wiley & Sons for their support, professionalism, and insightful feedback.

Last but not least, I would like to express my appreciation to Don Loney, Executive Editor of John Wiley & Sons Canada, for his patience and encouragement in the development of this book. I have had the pleasure of knowing Don for over 15 years. I have indeed been fortunate to work with such a consummate professional in the publishing business.

Preface

This book provides practical advice and step-by-step guidance to assist you in getting a mortgage for your home. By understanding the real estate market and what mortgage products are available and how they work, you will save money, enjoy the process of finding the right mortgage for your circumstances, and have the satisfaction of knowing that you have negotiated the "best deal."

This book is written from the perspective of a lawyer who has practised extensively in the area of Canadian real estate law for many years. This includes experience from acting for those involved in mortgage funding such as borrowers, lenders, buyers, sellers, developers, and investors; my own real estate investor experience over a 35-year period; and informal feedback from participants in my real estate seminars. I also conducted interviews with experts in the mortgage and financing industry in addition to other research.

Mortgages Made Easy is divided into two parts; the first is "Real Estate Basics," which covers understanding the real estate market, what features to look for in a single-family house or condo, determining the worth of the property, and selecting your real estate team.

The second part of the book is called "All about Mortgages." It covers types and sources of mortgages; costs involved in obtaining a mortgage; how large a mortgage is safe for you to carry; selecting the right mortgage for your needs; cost-saving ideas; implications of defaulting on your mortgage; and government-assistance programs. The second part also includes advice on mortgage helpers, financing options for seniors, creative financing, renewing, refinancing and renegotiating a mortgage, and investing in mortgages.

In the Appendix you will find information about mortgages as investment tools, a glossary, helpful websites, and forms and checklists.

I hope you enjoy this book and find the information helpful and encouraging. Your candid feedback on how this book can better meet your needs is welcomed and will assist in preparing future editions.

Please refer to the back of the book for contact information. You can provide input if you like, or request information on seminars relating to real estate in Canada. The website: www.homebuyer.ca has lots of practical articles, checklists, and helpful websites. It also has a free e-mail newsletter and other educational information.

Good luck and best wishes.

Douglas Gray,
Vancouver, B.C.
April 2006
www.homebuyer.ca

Introduction

Before You Think about Buying a Property. . .

For those of you who haven't owned a house or a piece of property, and aren't familiar with mortgages and financing, or those of you who presently own a house but find you need to relocate or want to buy a second property, you have this in common: a need to have a better understanding of how the world of purchase and financing operates. The axiom that knowledge is power is true. Knowing how to play the "mortgage/financing" game will have a positive and powerful impact on the end result. You will be able to select wisely from the options available to you and negotiate the best package for your needs. You will save money, time, and frustration on the one hand, and reduce risk, stress, and uncertainty on the other.

This introduction offers an overview of what to expect from this book and covers why you should (and perhaps why you shouldn't) consider owning a home or investment property. Although each chapter is self-contained, all should be read thoroughly because the concepts, tips, strategies, and pitfalls discussed are frequently interconnected.

WHY OWN REAL ESTATE?

There are many advantages to owning real estate, but also draw-backs. The advantages or benefits are discussed first.

Low Risk

Any investment has a potential risk, and you can indeed lose money in real estate. Real estate, though, has traditionally been a secure, stable investment compared to other investments, especially if you buy prudently. There are various reasons for the relatively low risk, which naturally will vary depending on the area where you buy.

The value of a property can rise because of a demand for housing, attractive financing rates, and the fact that land values consistently appreciate faster than rates of inflation. The market is cyclical so values will go up and down, but generally speaking, depending on location and other factors, real estate values increase over time.

You Don't Need a Lot of Starting Capital

You can enter the real estate market with a minimum amount of money, possibly 5% of the purchase price as a down payment, and borrow the rest of the money you need, using the property as security. For example, you could buy a $150,000 condominium, put 10% down, and finance the remaining 90%. Because you are borrowing more than 75% of the cost to purchase the property, this is called high-ratio financing, where the ratio between the debt (mortgage of 90%) and equity (your down payment of 10%) is high. (This is covered in more detail in Part II.)

Don't Be Afraid—You Can Get into the Market

Compared to other investments, such as investing in the stock market, buying your own home can be relatively easy. You don't need a lot of experience and the knowledge and skills can be learned, regardless of your education, age, or background. It just takes motivation, drive, and a desire to learn.

Using Leverage

Leverage means that you use a small amount of your own money and borrow the rest—other people's money (OPM). Wealth can be achieved by applying the simple principle of leverage. For example, financing 90% of a purchase is an example of a highly leveraged investment. Basically the ratio is 9:1; that is, nine times as much money is borrowed compared to what is invested. The risk, if the lender has to sell, is relatively minimal, in that the net proceeds after sale should at least cover the amount of the mortgage, especially considering the historical appreciation in value. There are exceptions, however.

If the property owner levers up the property too high (that is, has a high-ratio debt of say, 95%), and the market moves into a declining part of the cycle, then the owner and the lender could be at risk. That is why the higher the amount of the mortgage, the higher the risk for the lender and therefore the higher the interest rate, unless the mortgage is insured. For example, if you are buying a $200,000 house and have three mortgages—a first at $150,000, a second at $20,000 and a third at $10,000—the respective interest rates on those mortgages could be 6%, 9%, and 14%. The third mortgage carries the highest interest rate and has the highest risk because it is the last to be repaid upon sale of the home.

On the other hand, if you have a first mortgage that represents 90% of the purchase price, and it is insured against default and loss as a high-ratio mortgage, your interest rate could be the basic 6% to 7% (current rate at the time of writing). The two companies that insure high-ratio mortgages are CMHC (Canada Mortgage and Housing Corporation) and Genworth Financial Canada.

Here is another example to show the power of leverage. Let's say you purchase a house for $200,000, put down 10% ($20,000), and borrow 90% ($180,000). The home appreciates by 10% over a period of a year in a buoyant market. What would be the return on your original investment of $20,000? The answer is 100%. In other words, the increase in value of your home of $20,000 (10% appreciation of the $200,000 original price) is a 100% return on your down payment investment of $20,000. Conversely, if you paid cash for the house, that is, the full $200,000, your return on your original investment, due to appreciation of 10% over the year ($20,000), would be 10%.

APPRECIATION OF VALUE

Appreciation simply means the increase in value of the property over time. It is the growth in value of your original capital investment. In Canada, the national average has been approximately 6% per year over a long period of time. As a caution, it should be stressed that this figure is an average. Certain regions will perform below the average. Conversely, a well-selected, well-located, and well-maintained property in a growing community could perform higher than the average.

HOW YOU BUILD EQUITY IN A PROPERTY

When you make payments on your mortgage, you pay down the principal over time. As you reduce your debt, you are at the same time building up your equity, that is, the portion of your original house price that you no longer owe any debt on. (This is independent of the percentage increase in appreciation or value of the property.)

In practical terms, most people commonly refer to equity as the amount of value in the property that the person owns, free and clear of any debt. It is the amount of equity that a lender will lend further money on and place a mortgage on as security. In realistic terms, your true equity is what you would net upon sale, after all real estate commissions and closing costs are taken into account. Lenders realize this as well, which is why they generally do not like to lend on 100% of the equity in order to minimize risk and leave a margin for safety.

Owning Real Estate Is a Hedge Against Inflation

You know that inflation is the increasing cost of buying a product or service. On the flip side, it is the decrease in your purchasing power. An item that cost $5 ten years ago now costs $10 due to the effect of inflation. People on fixed incomes who are not indexed (increased) for inflation are very aware of the eroding purchasing power of the dollar. The inflation rate in Canada varies at different times of the year and in different regions across the country. At one time Canada had double-digit inflation, but current policies have kept inflation to single digits.

Naturally, the appreciation of the value of property over time includes an inflation factor. Historically, land appreciation value for residential homes has been about 3% to 4% greater than the inflation rate. Another benefit of real estate investing is that you are paying off the mortgage in inflated dollars. That is, you are probably getting more money now in terms of salary increases to pay off lesser-value money when you took out the original mortgage.

Tax Advantages of Owning Real Estate

There are tax advantages to owning real estate, whether as a principal residence or investment property. It would be hard to find an investment that has as many benefits as real estate. For example, all the interest you receive from your bank account, term deposit, or GIC (guaranteed investment certificate) is fully taxable as income. So, if you are obtaining interest of 6% (the nominal rate) on your deposit, and the inflation rate is 3%, the "effective" or "real" rate of return is 3%. If you are paying tax at a 35% rate (2% based on the 6% nominal rate), then effectively you have a 1% rate of return on your money. Real estate does suffer from these tax hits, so wisely investing in real estate—starting with the principal residence—is clearly an attractive form of investment.

Some of the key tax advantages of real estate investment include:

- Tax-free capital gain on your principal residence.
- Ability to write off principal residence suite rental income against your home-related expenses.
- Ability to write off a portion of a home-based business income against your home expenses (the home-based business could even be to manage your residential investment income, if you have other real estate investments—check with your accountant).
- Reduced tax rate of 50% of a capital gain from investment in real estate. Flow-through of losses from negative cash flow can be applied against other sources of income.
- Deduction of real estate property investment expenses against income. Write-off of depreciation of the building against income.

Income Potential

If you are investing in real estate, a prudent investment could result in a net positive cash flow income to you every month, that is, after all expenses and debt servicing have been taken into account. Not only could the income provide you with additional money, but the fact that you have a positive cash flow is one factor that automatically increases the value of income-producing real estate, sometimes very substantially. If you are buying a principal residence, you may decide to rent out part of the house to generate income (e.g., a basement suite, but check your local bylaws first to avoid hassles).

ATTRACTIVE RETURN ON INVESTMENT

For all the reasons outlined above, the potential for an attractive return on your investment—not only before tax but after tax—is clearly attractive in real estate. Bear in mind that it is not how much you make before tax, but what you are able to keep after tax that is the important investment criteria.

INCREASING DEMAND FOR LAND

Land is a finite commodity. Due to population increase and decreasing supply, real estate prices go up. Many communities have slow-growth or no-growth policies, because of the rapidly expanding needs for community services and public works. This restricts land made available for new development, causing existing land that is available for development to go up in value. Real estate is a commodity that the public needs. Other investment commodities are not so reliable because they do not constitute a public need and, therefore, demand. In addition, many people want to have a second home as a retreat, vacation property, or place of retirement. This creates further demand for land.

DISADVANTAGES OF REAL ESTATE OWNERSHIP

To provide some balance, there are some investment issues to owning real estate that may not be in effect in other forms of investments. These issues may be a factor in your decision to purchase real estate.

EMOTIONS SHOULDN'T PLAY A ROLE

Some people make decisions based on emotion, rather than sound preparation, knowledge, and objective assessment. This problem is particularly common when people buy their first home. Particular aspects of the property may prove very appealing—a new kitchen, mature landscaping—but leave emotions aside. The more knowledgeable you are, the better-quality decisions you will make.

LACK OF LIQUIDITY

This means that you can't convert your real estate investments into cash quickly, as far as a sale is concerned, because many factors have to be taken into account. You could have the option of borrowing on your property, though.

EXTENDED HOLDING PERIOD

Most real estate investments are held for long periods of time, for example, five to 10 years. You will have to wait, therefore, to get your return on your investment, when the cycle is in your favour.

IT TAKES TIME AND ENERGY

Planning for the purchase of your real estate and the process of the purchase requires time and effort. Advance planning and preparation will help lessen the time involved.

POTENTIAL RISK

Again, the potential of course exists, but with prudent and cautious decision-making and by following the tips and strategies outlined in this book, the risk should be minimal or nonexistent, in practical terms.

Lack of Accurate Comparisons

The very nature of real estate makes a standardized reference point for comparing two or more properties difficult. Each property is unique. On the other hand, there are rules of thumb and formulas that are effective, especially in combination, for determining the value of any real estate package. These are explained in detail later in this book.

Exposure to Government Control

Government at all levels does have an impact on real estate. There are government laws and regulations covering a wide range of areas, including planning, zoning bylaws, use of property, building codes and licences, rent controls, and environmental regulations. In addition, governments can expropriate and require rights of way. All these factors could certainly impact on your investment if you are investing in real estate. The best way to eliminate a potential problem is to avoid it to begin with. That is why you have to do your research thoroughly and obtain expert legal and tax advice, especially in the case of income you realize from real estate investment.

If you are thinking of buying real estate for investment, refer to my book *Making Money in Real Estate: The Canadian Guide to Profitable Investment in Residential Property*, Revised Edition, published by John Wiley & Sons Canada, Ltd. Also refer to the website www.home-buyer.ca.

Part I

REAL ESTATE BASICS

Chapter I

How the Real Estate Market Works

In order to have a better appreciation of how the real estate market operates, you need to understand the cycles and factors that influence prices and interest rates. No buying or selling decisions should be made without an accurate market assessment.

THE REAL ESTATE CYCLE

Real estate is a cyclical industry. As in any such industry, the cycle historically creates shortage and excess. This relates to the issue of supply and demand in the marketplace. Too much supply creates a reduction in value; too little supply creates an increase in value. It is important to understand that different provinces, regions, and communities may be at different points of the economic cycle. Knowing where your region is in terms of the cycle is crucial when making buying or selling decisions.

One of the reasons for the cycle is that many developers are entrepreneurial by nature and operate according to short-term planning. If financing and credit are available, developers tend to build without regard for the overall supply and demand. If a consequent glut occurs and the demand is soft, prices come down as houses and condominiums go unsold.

External factors that can affect the real estate cycle include the following:

GENERAL BUSINESS ECONOMIC CYCLES

The economy historically goes through periods of increased economic growth followed by recessionary periods. In any given cycle, the economic impact is greater in certain parts of the country than in others. In a recessionary period, people lose their jobs and have to put their homes on the market. Real estate prices become depressed as potential purchasers decide to wait until the economy is more secure.

It is difficult to know for certain when the economy will turn around, but various indicators should give you some insight. If the economy has been in a recession for a sustained period of time, there could be definite opportunities to buy. Once the economy comes out of a recession, prices tend to climb. Conversely, if the economy has been on a buoyant growth trend for an extended period of time, be very cautious in purchasing because a change in the cycle, and therefore a drop in real estate prices, could be imminent.

LOCAL BUSINESS CYCLE

Each local economy has its own cycle and factors that impact on real estate prices. These factors may not be greatly influenced by the general (provincial or national) business cycles just discussed.

COMMUNITY CYCLE

Certain geographic locations within a community can have their own economic cycles as well as supply and demand, all of which affect real estate prices. In addition, a community has its own life cycle from growth to decline to stagnation to rehabilitation. Look for areas of future growth.

As you can see, being aware of economic, business, and community cycles is critical to prudent decision-making. Before buying or selling real estate in a certain area, determine what external factors are prevalent and how they impact on the cycle of the real estate market. Different types of real estate—for example, condominiums, new houses, resale houses, and small apartment buildings—can be at different points of a cycle. You are undoubtedly familiar with the common terms used to describe the three types of real estate markets. As a brief review, they are:

SELLER'S MARKET

In a seller's market, the number of buyers who want homes exceeds the supply or number of homes on the market. In this type of market homes will sell quickly, prices will increase, and a large number of buyers are available for a minimal inventory of homes. These characteristics have implications for the buyer who has to make decisions quickly, must pay more, and frequently has his conditional offers rejected.

BUYER'S MARKET

In a buyer's market, the supply of homes on the market exceeds the demand or number of buyers. Homes will be on the market longer, fewer buyers will be available compared to the higher inventory of homes, and house prices will be reduced. The implications for buyers in this type of market are more favourable negotiating leverage, more time to search for a home, and better prices.

BALANCED MARKET

In a balanced market, the number of homes on the market is equal to the demand or number of buyers. Houses sell within a reasonable period, the demand equals supply, sellers accept reasonable offers, and prices are generally stable. The implications for the buyer in this type of market are that the atmosphere is more relaxed and there are a reasonable number of homes from which to choose.

FACTORS THAT AFFECT REAL ESTATE PRICES

There are many factors that influence the price of real estate. Whether you are a buyer or seller, you need to understand what factors are present that are impacting on the market, so you can make the right decisions at the right time and in the right location. Many of these factors are interconnected.

POSITION IN REAL ESTATE CYCLE

As described above, where the real estate market is in the cycle will have a bearing on prices.

INTEREST RATES

There is a direct connection between interest rates and prices. The higher the rates, the lower the prices. The lower the rates, the higher the prices. The lower the rates, the more people who can afford to buy their first home or an investment property. This puts pressure or greater demand on the market. A more detailed discussion of interest rates will follow below.

TAXES

High municipal property taxes can make a potential buyer think twice. So can provincial taxes, such as the property purchase tax. Federal tax legislation on real estate, such as changes in capital gains tax, could have a negative or positive influence on investors. All these factors affect real estate activity, including prices.

Rent Controls

Naturally, provincial rent controls and related restrictions could have a limiting effect on investor real estate activity, thereby resulting in fewer buyers in the market for certain types of properties.

The Economy

Confidence in the economy is important to stimulate home-buyer and investor activity. If the economy is buoyant and the mood is positive, more market activity will occur, generally resulting in price increases. Conversely, if the economy is stagnant, the opposite dynamic occurs, resulting in a decrease in activity and lower prices. If real estate purchasers are concerned about the same problem, a predictable loss of confidence occurs in the market.

Population Shifts

A region that has a booming economy and is attracting business, employment, and tourism will attract people. This means an increased demand for housing and a rise in prices. Conversely, a stagnant or declining economy will force real estate prices to drop.

Vacancy Levels

If there are high rental vacancy levels, this could impact investor confidence due to the risk of not finding tenants. On the other hand, if there are low vacancy levels, this could stimulate investor activity as well as first-time homebuyers. Renters who can't find a place to rent may borrow from relatives or find other creative ways to enable them to finance a home.

LOCATION

This is more than a cliché—it truly is an important factor. Properties in desirable locations will generally go up in price more quickly and consistently.

AVAILABILITY OF LAND

If there is a shortage of raw land, municipal zoning restrictions, limits on development, or provincial land-use laws that restrict the use of existing land for housing purposes, these factors will generally cause prices to increase. Again, it relates to the principle of supply and demand.

PUBLIC IMAGE

The public perception of certain geographic locations, certain types of residential properties (such as loft condominiums), or reputation of a builder will affect demand and therefore price. Some areas or types of properties are "hot" and some are not at any given time.

POLITICAL FACTORS

The policy of a provincial or municipal government in terms of supporting real estate development will naturally have a positive or negative effect on supply and demand, and therefore prices.

SEASONAL FACTORS

Certain times of year are traditionally slow months for residential real estate sales; hence prices decline. For example, November through February is usually a slow time. Conversely, interest in real estate starts to build as winter turns to spring, from March onward. People with children in school tend to want to make a purchase decision that closes during the summertime to avoid disruption of their children's schooling. The same seasonal factors impact on recreational property.

FACTORS THAT AFFECT MORTGAGE INTEREST RATES

There are many factors that impact on the rate of mortgage interest. Here are the key ones.

FEDERAL GOVERNMENT POLICY

The federal government, through the Bank of Canada (Central Bank), sets the prime bank rate. This is the rate that the Central Bank charges on loans to financial institutions. The rate is set each week at 25 basis points above the average yield (interest return) on three-month treasury bills. The government auctions these bills weekly. One hundred basis points represents 1.00% interest; therefore, 25 basis points would represent 0.25% interest. Conventional lenders (banks, trust companies, and credit unions) adjust their prime rates and mortgage rates using the federal bank rate as a guide. The Central Bank rate, therefore, sets a trend throughout the system. There are various factors and political/economic dynamics that influence the federal bank rate.

When you apply for a mortgage, you may wish to have a variable mortgage, or a six-month open mortgage, if you expect interest rates to go down. Then you can convert to a 3-, 5-, or 10-year closed mortgage when you see that interest rates are heading up. This is just one of many considerations you have to take into account when determining the kind of mortgage that meets your needs. (Other factors to consider will be discussed in Part II.)

Excess or Shortage of Supply of Money

Real estate cycles are connected to the general economic cycle. When lenders have an excess supply of money to lend due to an inflow of customer deposits (for example, at RRSP deadline time in the spring), interest rates tend to be more attractive and competitive. This is because the lender needs to make money; that is, a "spread" on the difference between what it pays the depositor and what it charges for lending money. This spread could be 1% to 2% or more depending on various factors, including competition.

> Lenders realize that borrowers want to get the best rate. Consumers track mortgage interest rates published in newspapers and on the Internet. They can—and should—comparison shop.

Depositors must earn enough money on their savings to be comparable to the returns that they would earn on other investments, relative to the same degree of risk and liquidity. The willingness of people to place money in a savings account is where the pool of mortgage money is created. When the inflow of deposit funds is high and the interest rates are low, the lender will have funds to lend. This scenario is referred to as a "loose money" market. In this situation, real estate activity can be expected to increase, as more people will be able to afford financing and purchase a home or other real estate investment. As there is more activity in the market place, there is a dynamic of supply and demand and real estate prices can be expected to rise.

On the other hand, if the public thinks it can get a better return on other forms of investment than putting their money in the bank in a low-interest situation, lenders will be left with a shortage of money to lend out for mortgages or other loans. This is referred to as a "tight money" market. Lenders may cut back on lending mortgage funds in many cases and be extra selective where the money is lent. Developers and contractors could have difficulty getting funds to build and therefore real estate activity slows down. As potential purchasers could have difficulty obtaining funds, they may choose to hold off on a purchase, so real estate prices could drop due to the reduced demand. If mortgage interest rates are too high, many people may not be able to afford to buy because they may not qualify for the amount of financing they need.

TYPE OF LENDER

Rates vary from lender to lender, depending on their policies and restrictions. A more conservative lender may charge a higher rate than another. In general terms, conventional lenders—banks, trust companies, and credit unions—tend to be fairly competitive in the rates they charge for mortgages. A private mortgage lender may take on more risk but will charge a higher rate.

QUALITY OF BORROWER

Lenders assess the creditworthiness of the borrower and the ability to pay. A borrower with few assets, who is recently employed or self-employed, or who has a spotty credit record, will pay a higher rate of interest than a borrower who has the opposite profile. For example, this is graphically reflected in the case of loans to a business. The lowest-risk/no-risk customer could receive the prime rate of interest (lowest) for a loan. Higher-risk businesses could be paying prime +1% to prime +8% or more, depending on the circumstances.

QUALITY OF PROPERTY

After the lender has appraised the property, assessed the type of location and resale potential of the property, and determined the amount of equity the borrower is putting in, the lender will set the mortgage rate. For properties that are recreational, rural, or speculative, or raw land, the lender will often require higher owner equity. Conversely, if you are buying a house or condominium in an economically stable community, you would probably be offered a competitive rate.

PRIORITY OF MORTGAGE

This issue is discussed in more detail in Part II. Basically, the security of the mortgage is greater depending on its date of registration relative to other mortgages. A mortgage that is registered first is referred to as a first mortgage; a mortgage that is registered second in line is referred to as a second mortgage; and so on. In the event that the borrower defaults on a mortgage and the property is sold, the first mortgage gets paid out first from the proceeds, followed by the second, etc. Therefore, the lower the mortgage ranks in terms of priority, the higher the risk to the lender that could potentially lose money if there is a shortfall on sale.

> There is a direct relationship between risk and interest rate. A first mortgage could be at 6%, a second at 10%, and a third at 15%. How much equity the owner has is also a factor in assessing risk. The larger the down payment, no matter how many mortgages on the property, the lower the risk to the lenders of losing money on a forced sale.

Terms of a Mortgage

While there is a more detailed discussion of mortgage terms in Part II, here are some key factors that affect the interest rate.

- The amortization period; that is, the length of time the mortgage is paid out in full.
- Whether the mortgage is insured by CMHC or Genworth Financial Canada. If there is a lower risk, there is a lower rate.
- The length of the term before the mortgage is due for payment or renegotiation (e.g., six months, five-years, or longer). Generally speaking, the longer the term, the more the risk of uncertainty of interest rates for the lender over that extended period and therefore the higher the rate, as a protective buffer. This is not always the case, however.
- Whether the mortgage is open, closed, or transferable. If it is open, it can be paid at any time before the end of the term without penalty—for instance, if you sell the house before the mortgage term is up. If closed, it cannot be repaid or can be repaid with a penalty (e.g., three months' interest or interest differential for the balance of the term, whichever is greater). Open mortgages have higher interest rates; closed mortgages have lower interest rates. A transferable mortgage means you have the right built into your original mortgage terms to transfer your mortgage to the new property you are buying at the time of sale, or within a certain time period after you sell, depending on the bank's criteria.
- Whether the interest rate is calculated and compounded annually, semi-annually, or monthly. The more frequent the interest calculation and compounding, the higher the effective rate of interest that you will be paying.

- The frequency of your payment schedule (e.g., weekly, bi-monthly, monthly, etc.).

Chapter 2

BUYING A HOUSE: THE FIRST STEPS

There are many types of residential real estate; deciding on which type to buy depends on many factors such as whether you are buying a home to live in (principal residence) or for investment purposes, and how much you can afford.

There are various single-family house choices available: buying a resale house, buying a new house, buying a lot and building a house yourself or with a builder, or assembling a pre-fabricated house. There are advantages and disadvantages to each option.

IF BUYING A RESALE HOUSE

Here are some of the advantages—and disadvantages—of buying a resale house rather than a new house. These guidelines are general in nature and will not necessarily apply in all cases.

ADVANTAGES

- Generally less expensive than a new house.
- Has character or a "lived-in" feeling.
- May have a unique architectural style.

- Any structural problems (e.g., settling, cracks in the walls, etc.) will be picked up by the home inspector.
- Landscaping is usually mature.
- Neighbourhood is established and has developed its own character.
- Community services are established.
- May include extras not normally included in a new home purchase, such as customized features that previous owners have built or installed.
- No GST applies to the purchase.

DISADVANTAGES

- The resale house may not have been built according to existing building standards or codes (e.g., aluminum rather than copper wiring, lead rather than copper pipes, inefficient insulation or urea formaldehyde foam insulation [UFFI], etc.) and may need upgrading.
- Buyers of new homes may be protected by a provincial New Home Warranty Plan; such protection is not available to resale purchasers.
- If a resale house is in a metropolitan area, the price could be inflated because of the higher value of land, whereas a new house in a suburban area could be less expensive due to lower cost of land.
- An older home may have been renovated by the owner or a handyman without a building permit and inspection; therefore, the safety or functional aspects of the house could be deficient.
- Some older homes do not have an attractive or functional design (e.g., rooms may be too small or laid out poorly),

have low-ceiling basements that make that area less functional for comfortable use or use as a rental suite, have
small or old-fashioned bathrooms and kitchens, etc. To
substantially renovate an older house can be expensive and
time-consuming.
• The systems (e.g., heating and cooling) may be outdated and
need repair, and appliances could be older and perhaps worn
and lack modern features.

IF BUYING A NEW HOUSE

You may wish to purchase a new house for your principal residence or as an investment. Here are some of the advantages and
disadvantages of buying a new house over an older resale house.

Advantages

• A newly built house tends to be better designed in terms of
room layout (e.g., large kitchen, extra bathrooms, en suites),
functional purpose (e.g., higher ceilings in basement, patio,
family room), and brighter atmosphere (e.g., larger windows, skylights).
• A builder may offer several house models for buyers to choose
from. You generally can customize certain features. Optional
or standard features you may be able to customize include
carpet colour and material, kitchen appliance colours, kitchen
and bathroom floor coverings, paint colours, etc.
• The house has been constructed in compliance with current
building code standards (e.g., plumbing, electrical, heating,
insulation, etc.) and is clean, modern, and fresh.
• You will be the first occupant in the house, which for some
people is a plus because you can personalize the house to

meet personal or family needs, rather than working with a previous owner's design taste.

- Market valuation of the house is easier to do because of similar comparables built in the same area.
- You can get more house for the money compared to a resale house if the new house is built in a suburb where land costs are comparatively lower.
- Many new homes are built by builders who are registered with the New Home Warranty Program in their province. Therefore, if problems occur after the sale is complete and if the specific problems are covered by the program, the builder will correct them. Check with your provincial New Home Warranty Program.

DISADVANTAGES

- The builder may not be registered with the New Home Warranty Program, so there might not be an obligation for the builder to fix problems should they occur.
- Many new home developments are built a considerable distance from the city core, so commuting time increases. There may also be a lack of certain services common to established areas.
- It is not uncommon to have construction delays (e.g., paving of driveways, landscaping, other finishing touches) and defects to be fixed, both of which cause frustration and possible expense.
- Many new-home buyers purchase from plans or an artist's sketch or model plans. Unless your builder has constructed a model home, you are left to conceptualize how your house will feel.

- Purchase documents prepared by the builder tend to be more complex and detailed compared to resale house contracts. (This is discussed shortly.)
- GST must be paid on new-home purchases. A substantially renovated house could be deemed to be a new home for the purpose of GST. A partial rebate could be available in both cases. Check with the builder, your lawyer, and the local GST office.
- The deposit funds you pay to the company could be lost if the builder goes bankrupt. In some provinces there is consumer protection legislation that protects these funds. Unless you put the funds in a lawyer's or realtor's trust account, though, you could lose your deposit. It is particularly important that you check out the builder's reputation. Here are some guidelines:

  - Research the New Home Warranty Program in your province: This could be a provincial program or private program. If the builder is registered with the New Home Warranty Program, in some provinces the deposit funds are protected up to a maximum amount. If the builder is not registered with NHWP, be very cautious and don't pay any money or sign a builder's contract without your lawyer's advice. The NHWP programs for each province are basically similar. The builder adds the fee for NHWP coverage to the house price or builds it into the price. NHWP coverage generally includes buyer protection for the deposit, incomplete work allowance, warranty protection up to a year, basement protection for two years, and major structural defect protection for five years. Although the NHWP is designed to protect purchasers of newly constructed houses (condominiums can also be covered) against defects in construction, there are limitations in coverage. These limitations and exclusions could cost you a lot of money. That is why you need to check out the NHWP and builder thoroughly.

- Contact the local or provincial Home Builders' Association (see Appendix for addresses).
- Check with the local Better Business Bureau, where any complaints against the contractor will be registered.
- Contact purchasers of houses from other developments the contractor has built. Ask for the names of past customers as references for you to contact. Also ask the contractor to give you names and locations of previous development projects. You can then randomly knock on doors and ask the owners if they would give you their candid opinion as to the quality of the house and whether the builder corrected any problems to the owners' satisfaction. Ask the purchaser if they got the value they paid for. A key question to ask is, "Would you buy from the same builder again, and why or why not?"
- Check with the local (municipal) business licensing office to verify that the contractor is licensed.

If the contractor has no previous history or record in the industry, be very cautious. The contractor could have been operating under a previous company name that went under and is now operating under a different company name. Alternatively, the contractor could be a first-timer and be learning at your expense. Take the time to check out the contractor. It will save you time, frustration, and money later on.

The Builder's Contract

Make sure that you take the contract supplied by the house builder to your lawyer before you sign it. For obvious reasons, builders' contracts are written to favour the builder. Sometimes you can negotiate changes to the contract; other times you cannot. It depends on the builder, the nature of the changes, and the market (hot or soft). Occasionally there are terms that the builder must be flexible on if the purchaser's lawyer finds them unfair. The builder may alter these terms to close the deal.

Key Contract Items

- **Deposit Money.** Is the deposit money going to be held in trust, and where? Is interest going to be paid on the deposit to the credit of the purchaser? There is a risk if the money is going directly to the builder and is not being held in trust by a lawyer or real estate company.
- **Financing.** Is the builder going to arrange financing at a fixed rate through a lender or carry the financing himself? Make sure the payment terms are clearly spelled out. Check to make sure the rates and terms are competitive and that the financing package is attractive. For example, the builder could provide or arrange for a discounted interest rate for a year. The rate could be artificially low, rather than a prevailing market rate, to attract buyers who might not otherwise be interested or qualify for financing. What if interest rates go up when it comes time for you to refinance? Will you be able to handle the increased monthly payments?

- **Assigning or Selling**. Does the builder's contract have a restriction in it preventing you from assigning your interest in the contract to someone else before the closing date, or selling your property to someone else after closing, within a certain period of time? Some builders will not want you to assign before closing so that you make a potential profit in a "hot" market. Other builders will not want you to resell your property after closing and before they have sold out the rest of the project; otherwise, they could lose a potential sale, or you could offer your house for sale at a lower price, thereby affecting their pricing structure.
- **Closing Date**. What if the builder does not close on the agreed date? Consider adding clauses to the effect that the house price will be reduced by an agreed sum for each day the builder is late, giving the purchaser the option to back out of the contract and get his deposit money back, plus accrued interest, if the purchaser so wishes (you might not want to exercise this option with a fixed sale price in an escalating market). Or you could add your own penalty clause that the builder has to pay you if the building is not completed on time (for example, an agreed amount of credit toward your purchase price for each week of delay).

Depending on your needs and objectives, always ask your lawyer to advise you. Attempt to negotiate a better deal. If you are not satisfied with the outcome, consider buying from a different builder.

IF BUYING A LOT AND BUILDING A HOUSE

Some people prefer to buy a section of land and hire a contractor to build the house, or build it themselves, or buy a modular home (e.g., log cabin, ski chalet, etc.) and have it put together.

Make sure, if you are building your own house, that you know what you are doing; otherwise, the effort will become massively time-consuming, frustrating, and expensive. It might be advisable to take a course on building a house and then hire a contractor you trust on an hourly basis to advise you.

Check with your municipal planning department on the building codes, permits, and inspections required. There are many regulations involved. Read how-to books on building your own house. You could save money and enjoy doing it yourself, but don't overestimate your abilities or the amount of time you have available. Do-it-yourself construction almost always turns out to be more complicated, time-consuming, and lengthy than initially expected.

> Many of the problems that do-it-yourselfers have in their dealings with contractors are due to misunderstanding of the rights, responsibilities, and functions of the various people who are involved in the work. Be clear on your responsibilities for oversight of the project, and those of the contractor and tradesmen.

Working with a Contractor

It is important to be clearly focused on what your needs are before you commit to taking on such a large project. You should have at least three competitive bids (written fixed-price quotes) from contractors before selecting the one you want.

Check on the reputation and past performance of the contractor (refer to the previous section on "Buying a New House"). This is very important. Also, consider the advantages of hiring a contractor who is registered with the New Home Warranty Program. You will pay an extra amount for this coverage protection, but the benefits are obvious. Ask the contractor who his insurance company is and ask for written verification that he has adequate public liability and property damage insurance. Verify with the insurance company if you have any doubts or concerns.

As mentioned earlier, it is essential that you have a written contract with the contractor. Many homebuilder associations have sample contracts available that you can use, so check with them. Make sure you have your lawyer look at the contract, and involve your lawyer in the release of any monies that are paid to the contractor as the work progresses. Depending on the nature of the house construction, there could be from three to five different payments at various stages of construction.

At each stage verify that the work is complete, and ideally that the sub-trades, suppliers, etc., have been paid, and that there is nothing outstanding from a previous payment (also called a "draw"). It is not uncommon for contractors to pay for services performed by sub-trades or supplies purchased from suppliers from each progress draw. "Lien searches" are carried out by your lawyer to make sure that no liens have been filed before the payment is made.

Your lender will normally require that progress draws be made. This is the normal custom. You can see the problem that could occur if you give too much money to the builder without the necessary work in kind being performed. The contractor could go out of business or just not perform the work, and you could be out the money advanced.

The usual terms found in a construction contract include the following:

- Date of agreement.
- Correct and complete address of the property where the work will be done.
- Your name and address.
- Contractor's name, address, and telephone number. If a company name is used, the name of the company's official on-site representative should be indicated.
- Detailed description of the work, sketches, and list of materials to be used.
- The type of work that will be subcontracted.
- The right to retain a builder's lien holdback as specified under provincial law.
- A clause stating that work will conform to the requirements of all applicable federal, provincial, or municipal building codes.
- Start and completion dates.
- The contracted price and payment schedule (remember the lien holdback, normally 10%).
- An agreement on who is responsible for obtaining all necessary permits, licences, and certificates.
- A clause setting out the procedures for confirming in writing any "extras" to the contract requested by the owner.
- Signatures of the parties to the contract.

IF BUYING A PROPERTY FOR RENOVATION

There are many types of residential properties that would see a rise in value if renovated. Generally speaking, single-family houses and multi-unit dwellings fall into this category. If you are buying for a principal residence, the considerations below apply. If you are considering buying a property as an investment, the strategy is to find the right property, improve it, raise rents to increase the value, and sell at the right time for maximum profit.

If you are buying a property to renovate as your principal residence, here are some factors to consider:

- Look for a neighbourhood where houses are being upgraded. This is a signal of rising values and a neighbourhood that is attracting investment.
- The region/neighbourhood should be serviced by various forms of transportation.
- The neighbourhood should be an attractive one, well kept, where houses reflect pride of ownership. Assess the area's crime rate.
- The property to be renovated should be in a neighbourhood that is not yet in high demand, generally speaking.
- New construction of commercial areas (e.g., a shopping centre) or other nearby existing commercial areas is a positive sign.
- The property should ideally have some character and quality construction and craftsmanship.
- Ideally, the property should be close to other attractive draws that enhance the general area, such as rapid transit, a college or university, parks, libraries, or waterfront.
- The property should have the potential for renovation and approved zoning from City Hall.
- Look for a community organization that is striving to improve the quality of the neighbourhood; this is a positive sign in terms of pride and initiative.

Before you buy a property that you are considering for renovation, either to live in, or rent out, here are some tips:

- Make sure that you understand the renovation process. If you are not experienced in this area, get expert advice.
- Be realistic and focused on the types of renovations and types of renovation properties you are considering. Certain types of renovations get a better return on your investment in terms of price and general saleability. The highest return generally comes from renovating the kitchen and bathrooms.
- Make sure that your personal goals and investment goals are clear. Do you intend to purchase a property as a principal residence and then renovate it throughout the year and sell it? If so, you would normally be exempt from paying any capital gains tax on sale, because it would be deemed your principal residence.
- Compare various properties and draw up a shortlist of two or three that have good potential profit return. That way you can negotiate with more leverage because you are not interested in just one property.
- Consider having an architect view the property and give you ideas on how the property can be improved.
- Have a professional appraiser give you an idea of the current market value.
- Have a professional building inspector give you a report on the physical aspects, internally and externally, of the building, including what potential changes would be possible.
- Have several contractors, ideally a minimum of three, give you written quotes on the cost of doing the renovations that you want.

IF YOU ARE BUYING A RECREATIONAL PROPERTY

For many reasons, the demand for recreational property has grown dramatically in some parts of Canada. Whether you are looking at buying recreational property for personal use or as an investment, the purchase has the potential to deliver an attractive financial return.

The term "recreational property" refers to a range of properties, including an existing building (chalet, cabin, cottage, etc.), a building lot, or a hobby farm, with recreational amenities and pursuits nearby. In broad terms, a recreational property could also be a condominium or townhouse. Various trends are driving interest in rural or recreational property:

- People have more leisure time.
- There is a preference for an enhanced quality of life to provide balance from a hectic urban or metropolitan-based career, or from expense and time involved in commuting.
- The best aspects of country and city life are combined.
- Some people are opting to run a business from a more rural site or telecommuting (e.g., using telecommunications to interact with one's employer).
- The dream of having a family retreat, which could possibly be passed on to succeeding family generations.
- Desire to have a future retirement home.
- Recreational properties are less expensive to purchase, in general terms, than urban or metropolitan properties.
- Increase in demand (and therefore value) for recreational or rural property that is proximate (within four-hour driving distance) to a metropolitan or urban population growth area.

- The possibility that the vendor would be more likely to carry financing (e.g., provide a "vendor-take-back" mortgage to the purchaser).
- The possibility that the vendor would consider giving you an "option to purchase" the property for a period of time (e.g., one to two years at an agreed price; the option fee itself is normally nominal).

There are some potential downsides to purchasing recreational property. These are general comments, however, and there are many exceptions.

- Lenders are sometimes reluctant to lend money or approve a mortgage for recreational property, especially raw land. However, CMHC has recently changed its lender criteria to provide high-ratio financing for recreational property. You have options to deal with this issue:

  - Increase your down payment to meet the lender's financing limit.
  - Raise a mortgage on the equity of your present home to buy the recreational property.
  - Have the bank put a "blanket" mortgage on both your current home and recreational property.
  - Attempt to have the vendor finance you by means of a first or second mortgage on the property.
  - Purchase the property with friends, family, or other investors.

- There may be some restrictions on land use. (This will be discussed below.)

- Maintenance of the property could be frustrating if you are far from home.
- Vandalism is more likely if the property is in a remote location or is used only seasonally.
- If the economy is in a recession, the value of property can diminish if you need to sell, as the demand for recreational property is generally considered a luxury and not a necessity.

There are special considerations when assessing recreational property for purchase. Here are some issues to consider specific to recreational or rural property:

- *Location.* This is one of the most important aspects. You want to consider proximity to your home and consequent travelling time, what unique features are present (such as tourist attractions or the area's natural beauty), desirability of location relative to other areas, and whether the area has seasonal or year-round usage.
- *Accessibility.* The convenience of reaching the area is important (e.g., by ferry, boat, plane, car, etc.) within a reasonable time, plus excellent access to and on the property.
- *Restrictions on Use.* Your lawyer must search the title of the property in the land registry office to see what encumbrances may be on title, as a condition of any offer you make.
- *Right of Way.* This generally means a statutory (legal) right for certain companies, Crown corporations, or government departments to use or have access to part of your property. Examples would be for hydro, telephone, sewer, drainage, dike, or public-access purposes.
- *Easement.* An easement is similar to a right of way, but is the term often used when one neighbour gives another neighbour

the right to use or have access to a piece of land (e.g., permission to reach a waterfront by crossing a neighbour's land). This agreement is put into writing and filed in the respective land registry office.

- *Restrictive Covenant.* In this situation, a developer in a recreation-property subdivision could make any purchase subject to an ongoing restriction in certain areas (e.g., requiring that all roofs be covered by cedar shakes rather than asphalt shingles). The purpose would be for aesthetic uniformity. A document setting out the restrictions would be filed in the land registry office.

- *Zoning.* There could be restrictions on the type of use of your property (e.g., seasonal use only, no mobile homes on the property, no other buildings to be constructed, etc.).

- *Leasehold Interest.* In this situation, the holder of the interest in land has the right to use the land for a fixed period of time, for example, 50 or 99 years. The owner of the property (landlord or lessor) signs an agreement with the holder of the leasehold interest (tenant or lessee) setting out various terms and conditions of the relationship. The leasehold contract would set out such conditions as maintenance requirements, restrictions on use of the land, building construction or renovation requirements, and other matters. A leasehold situation can cover condominiums or houses on residential or recreational property.

- *Government Land.* You might be interested in acquiring recreational property owned by the government. In the case of federal and provincial government ownership, it is referred to as Crown land. The land could also be owned by a municipality. The land can be leased or in some cases purchased outright. Whether it is leased or purchased, there could be restrictions on the nature of use.

- *Potable Water.* This is a critical issue. Does the property have public water or a well? Is the water safe to drink? Is it sufficient for your needs? If you don't have a well, what will it cost to drill one?
- *Waste Disposal.* What type of system is required or available? Is it a septic tank or other type of system? Is the soil suitable for a septic field? What about other types of waste disposal, such as garbage, etc.?
- *Crime.* Find out about the incidence of vandalism, theft, or arson in the area. Talk to the local police detachment.
- *Land Boundary.* Check to make sure that the boundaries of your property have been clearly marked and pegged by a surveyor. This is especially important with acreage or waterfront property. You don't want to have disputes with your neighbours.
- *Amenities.* What public or private recreational facilities are near the area you are considering? If the developer is establishing facilities, check out other projects by the developer to determine quality and satisfaction.
- *Local Government.* Make inquiries as to the attitude of the local government towards seasonal residents. Possibly a higher tax base is assessed to keep the tax base of year-round residents lower.
- *Existing Building.* If you are buying a property with an existing building on it (a home, chalet, or cottage), have the building inspected for its structural condition. The natural elements aside, if the building has not been properly maintained, it can deteriorate rapidly. Have the building checked for insect infestation, wood rot, etc.

Chapter 3

Why Buying a Condominium Is a Different Animal

Picked up a newspaper lately? Or lifestyle magazine? Condominiums are immensely popular both as a principal residence and as an investment. It can be said that condominium living may not be right for everyone, though, since it involves individual ownership in the unit and shared ownership in other property, as well as adherence to rules and regulations, and shared oversight. On the other hand, many people prefer condominium living over other alternatives.

WHAT IS A CONDOMINIUM?

The word "condominium" does not imply a specific structural form, but a legal form. Condominiums (called co-proprietorships in Quebec) may be detached or semi-detached houses, row-houses, stack townhouses, duplexes, or apartments. They can even be building lots, subdivisions, or mobile home parks. Whatever the style, a residential unit is specified and is owned by an individual in a freehold or leasehold format. The rest of the property, including land, called the "common elements," is owned in common. For example, the condo owner would own a fractional share of the common elements in the development. If there are 50 condominium owners, then each individual owner would own 1/50th as tenants-in-common of the common elements.

Condominiums can be built on freehold or leasehold properties. A condominium can also be in a stratified format, where a legal description for the unit is allocated in a vertical dimension. In other words, if you live in a condominium apartment on the 30th floor, there is a precise legal description in the land registry office for that specific unit in the complex. Another form is a bare land condominium. In this example, it would be similar to a building lot subdivision with individual units owned by the unit holders, although the units would appear as detached homes. The rest of the land would be considered common elements.

A condominium development is administered by various legal structures set out in provincial legislation.

> The legislation of each province can vary, but it is always designed to provide the legal and structural framework for the efficient management and administration of each condominium project. Once the condominium project documents are registered, the project is brought into legal being.

The part of the condominium that you will own outright is referred to as the "unit" in most provinces. You will have full and clear title to this unit when you purchase it (assuming you are buying a freehold, not a leasehold, property), which will be legally registered in your name in the land registry office in your province. The precise description of the common elements, and exactly what you own as part of your unit, may differ from development to development, but in any event this description will be included in the documents prepared and registered for each condominium.

Common elements generally include walkways, driveways, lawns and gardens, lobbies, elevators, parking areas, recreational facilities, storage areas, laundry rooms, stairways, plumbing, electrical systems, and portions of walls, ceilings and floors, and other items. Part of the common elements may be designated for the exclusive use of one or more of the individual unit owners, in which case these are called "limited common elements." In other words, they are limited for the use only of specific owners. Examples would include parking spaces, storage lockers, roof gardens, balconies, patios, and front and back yards.

DIFFERENT TYPES OF CONDOMINIUMS

RESIDENTIAL CONDOMINIUMS

Residential condominiums can be found in either a city or suburban setting. In an urban setting, the most common formats are as follows:

- A high-rise apartment building.
- A new, mid-rise (three- to five-storey) building.
- A converted older building that formerly consisted of rental apartments.
- A building where the street level floor is owned jointly by the condominium corporation members (the unit owners) and is rented out to retailers to help offset the common maintenance fees of the residential condominiums in the rest of the building.

- Same format as the previous one, except that the retail space is sold as condominiums.

In a suburban setting, the most common formats are as follows:

- Cluster housing consisting of multi-unit structures, using housing of two or four units apiece, each with its own private entranceway.
- Townhouses or single-family homes constructed in rows.
- Garden apartments consisting of a group of apartment buildings surrounding a common green space; often each floor is owned by an individual owner.
- A series of detached single-family homes in a subdivision format, all utilizing the same land and parking areas.
- Duplexes, triplexes, or fourplexes.

The suburban condominium format tends to make maximum use of the land while creating attractive views, private driveways, and common recreational facilities such as swimming pools, tennis courts, saunas, playground, etc. Many residential condominium developments, with the conveniences and amenities being offered, have created a complete lifestyle experience. The purpose of these separate developments—such as restaurants, shopping centres, recreational and entertainment facilities, and care facilities for seniors—is to make the condominium community a very distinct and self-contained environment for people with diverse interests and needs.

RECREATIONAL/RESORT CONDOMINIUMS
Recreational condominiums can take various forms, including mobile home parks where the "pad" with utility hookups is

owned in fee simple (which means that you own the title to the property outright; it is not on leased property) with a share in the common property of the rest of the park. Alternatively, it could be in a leasehold format. Another option is a bare land condominium in rural, wilderness, or waterfront areas. In these examples, an owner could build a cabin with fee-simple ownership of the land and own a partial interest in the common elements. The common elements could include a marina, beach, farm, or forest. Common recreational facilities could include a playground or community centre, and assets may include boats or farm animals.

The development of condominiums in resort areas is extensive, and condominiums are frequently built on lakeshores, sea coasts or island resorts, or in ski country. There are two main types of resort condominiums: those developed for warmer climates and those developed for winter climates.

Purchasers of a recreational or resort condominium tend to do one of the following:

- Own it outright and use it throughout the year.
- Own it outright and rent it when they are not using it.
- Own a portion of the condominium as a timeshare and use it for one week or more a year; normally each one-week block purchased is equivalent to approximately 1/50th ownership in the condominium.

ADDITIONAL EXPENSES RELATING TO CONDOMINIUM OWNERSHIP

Once you own a condominium unit, there are ongoing monthly or annual expenses and potential expenses that you have to plan for. People frequently don't take into consideration the extra expenses involved because of the difference from a more familiar single-family home situation. The most common additional expenses that you should be aware of, other than mortgage payments, are as follows.

PROPERTY TAXES

Each individual condominium unit is assessed by the municipality and therefore the owner(s) has to pay property taxes. If you have a mortgage, the lender may ask you to include extra monthly payments along with your mortgage. These are held in a property tax account so that the lender can pay your municipal property taxes. If you do not have a mortgage you will have to pay property tax separately. The common elements incur a property tax as well, but that tax is covered in your monthly maintenance payments.

MAINTENANCE PAYMENTS

Maintenance payments or "assessments for common expenses" cover all of the operating costs of the common elements and are adjusted according to any increase or decrease in expenses. You are responsible for a portion of the development's total operating costs. The formula for determining your portion is discussed below.

Unit entitlement is the basis on which the owner's contribution to the common expenses or maintenance fees of the condominium corporation are calculated. Various formulas are used for the calculation. In some developments the percentage calculated for the unit's share is determined by the original purchase price of each unit in relation to the value of the total property. Another method is to apportion costs on the basis of the number of units in equal proportion, regardless of unit size. But the most common formula is to calculate the unit entitlement by dividing the number of square feet in an owner's unit by the total square footage of all the units. For example, let's say a condominium development contains 15 condominium units. The total square footage of all units is 15,680. Your individual unit is 784 square feet, and the annual cost to maintain the common elements and other related expenses is $40,000. To calculate your monthly financial commitment you would go through the following steps:

- Calculate the unit entitlement (15,680 divided by 784 = 1/20 share in the common property)
- Calculate the annual share of maintenance costs ($40,000 x 1/20 = $2,000 per year)
- Calculate the monthly share of maintenance costs ($2,000 x 1 / 12 = $166.66 per month)

The payments for common expenses are made directly to the condominium corporation and generally cover the following items:

Maintenance and Repair of Common Property
This includes costs for maintenance, landscaping, building repairs, recreational facilities, equipment, and other expenses.

Operating and Service Costs
This includes expenses relating to garbage removal, heat, hydro, and electricity.

Contingency Reserve Fund
This is a fund for emergency problems and expenses that are not specifically allowed for in the budget (e.g., the roof needs repair, the swimming pool liner needs replacing, or the heating/cooling system is breaking down).

Owners contribute monthly to this fund on the basis of a portion of the monthly maintenance fee. The condominium legislation in most provinces requires a minimum amount to be contributed to the contingency reserve fund (e.g., 10% of annual budget). If you are buying an older condominium, you should check to see what percentage of the monthly payments is being allocated toward this fund, as there is a higher risk of needing to use the fund in older buildings than in new developments. In older buildings, the fund should be 25% or more, depending on the circumstances. In most cases you are not entitled to a refund of your contribution to the reserve fund when you sell your unit.

Management Costs
These are the costs associated with hiring private individuals or professional management firms to administer all or part of the daily functions of the condominium development.

Insurance
Condominium legislation requires that the development carry sufficient fire and related insurance to replace the common property in the event of fire or other damage. Condominium corporations generally obtain further insurance to cover other payables and liabilities. The insurance does not cover the damage done to the interior of an individual unit.

SPECIAL ASSESSMENT
There could be situations in which a large majority (75% or more) of the condominium members wish to raise funds for special purposes. These funds would not come from the contingency reserve fund or from the regular monthly assessments. For

example, there could be an interest in building a swimming pool or tennis courts, or it may be necessary to cover costs of repairs beyond the contingency reserve fund. If the decision is made to assess members, and the assessment has been properly approved, you cannot refuse to pay the special assessment, even though you might not agree with its purpose.

YOUR OWN INSURANCE

As mentioned earlier, the insurance on the building that is covered by the condominium development does not include the interior of your unit. Therefore, you will need to get separate insurance to cover the contents as well as damage to the inside of your unit, including walls, windows, and doors. There are several types of insurance, including replacement cost, all-risk comprehensive, and personal liability. It is a good idea to get insurance to cover deficiencies in the condominium corporation's insurance coverage in the event of fire so that any damage to your unit could be repaired in full; otherwise, the unit owners would have to pay any deficiency on a proportional basis by means of a special assessment. Many insurance companies offer a specialized program referred to as condominium homeowners package insurance.

LEASE PAYMENTS

If you have a leasehold condominium, you will be required to make monthly lease payments in addition to many of the other costs outlined in this section.

UTILITIES

You are responsible for the utilities that you use in your unit, including hydro, water, heat, etc. In apartment condominiums these expenses are usually included in the maintenance fee, whereas townhouse condominiums tend to be separately metered and you are billed directly and individually by the utility companies.

UNIT REPAIR AND MAINTENANCE COSTS

You will have to allocate a certain amount of your financial budget to repair and maintenance needs relating to the inside of your unit. Your monthly maintenance fee would cover common elements outside your unit only.

ADVANTAGES AND DISADVANTAGES OF CONDOMINIUM OWNERSHIP

In any situation of shared ownership and community living there are advantages and disadvantages. If you are only renting out the condominium, some of the following points may not be as important to you as if you were living in it.

ADVANTAGES

- Ready availability of financing as a single-family home.
- Range of prices, locations, types of structures, sizes, and architectural features available.
- Amenities such as swimming pools, tennis courts, health clubs, community centres, saunas, hot tubs, exercise rooms, sun decks, etc.
- Benefits of home ownership in terms of participation in the real estate market and potential growth in equity.
- Individual ownership of living units.
- Enables people of moderate and middle income to own their own home.
- Freedom to decorate interior of unit to suit personal tastes.
- Round-the-clock building security.
- Elimination of many of the problems of upkeep and

maintenance often associated with home ownership, since maintenance is usually the responsibility of a professional management company or manager.

- Often considerably cheaper than buying a single-family home because of more efficient use of land and economy of scale.
- Investment opportunity for profit if selected carefully.
- Good transitional type of home between rental apartments and single-family houses for growing families or singles or couples; conversely, good transition for "empty nesters" who wish to give up their larger family house.
- Reduction of costs due to responsibilities for repair and maintenance being shared.
- Elected council that is responsible for many business and management decisions.
- Participation of owners in the operation of the development, which involves playing a role in budget-setting and approval, decision-making, determination of rules, regulations and bylaws, and other matters affecting the democratic operation of the condominium community.

DISADVANTAGES

- Real estate appreciation is usually slower than for single-family homes (it is land that goes up in value).
- It may be difficult to accurately assess the quality of construction of the project.
- Members need to stick to bylaws, which might be confining for some (e.g., restriction on the right to rent, restriction on pets, etc.).
- People live closer together, thereby potentially creating problems from time to time. Frequent problem areas include the "Five P's": pets, parking, personality, parties, and people.

- If one needs to sell for fast cash, understand that condominiums generally take more time to market and sell than single-family houses. This is not always the case, of course; it depends on variables.
- One could be paying for maintenance and operation of amenities that one has no desire or intention to use.
- Management of the condominium council is by volunteers, who may or may not have the appropriate abilities and skills.
- Owners may be apathetic, so that the same people continually serve on council.
- Some elected councils behave in an autocratic fashion.

For more information about condominiums, refer to my book, *101 Streetsmart Condo Buying Tips for Canadians*, published by John Wiley & Sons Canada, Ltd. Also refer to the website www.homebuyer.ca.

Chapter 4

IS THE PRICE RIGHT?

How can you be sure a house is worth the advertised price? In theory, a property is worth whatever a buyer is prepared to pay. You can feel more certain about the value of any given property by learning and using appraisal techniques, or by purchasing the services of professional, qualified appraisers. In addition, there are "rules of thumb" that real estate investors often use to calculate the worth of a revenue property. These rules should only be considered approximations; for an investment property, always get an accurate and professional appraisal.

Appraising a property's value is more an art than a science. Two pieces of property are seldom identical. There are distinct benefits to having an appraisal done—for both a buyer and a seller—as it can help you to determine the following:

- A reasonable offering price for purchase of the property.
- The value of a property for financing purposes (your lender will require this).
- The value of a property when converting the use from principal residence to investment (rental) use, or vice versa. This would be for Canada Revenue Agency capital gains determination purposes, unless you are exempt from this provision. Check with your accountant for more details.

- A reasonable asking price when selling the property.
- The amount of insurance to carry.

> There are several professional designations for property appraisers in Canada. They subscribe to uniform academic, professional, and ethical standards, and are regulated by their professional associations. The most common national designations are AACI (Accredited Appraiser Canadian Institute) and CRA (Canadian Residential Appraiser). There are other national and provincial appraisal designations as well as specialty appraisal areas (e.g., industrial and commercial).

HOW A PROPERTY'S VALUE IS APPRAISED

Here are some of the basic methods or rules of thumb used by professional appraisers, real estate lenders, and homebuyers. If you are buying a home to live in, you will usually need only the market comparison approach and cost approach. The average of these two estimates is what most lenders use for appraisal purposes. The lender then provides mortgage funds based on the purchase price or appraised value, whichever is lower. The purchaser pays for the appraisal cost (usually between $150 and $300 for the average house or condominium purchase), but the lender arranges for the appraisal. Sometimes the lender also pays for the appraisal cost, for competitive goodwill purposes. Make a point of asking the lender to cover this cost.

If you intend to buy real estate as an investment rather than as your principal residence, there are many additional formulas to apply to determine the value of revenue property, but they are outside the scope of this book. If you are interested in investment real estate and evaluation criteria, refer to my book *Making Money in Real Estate: The Canadian Guide to Profitable Investment in Residential Property*, Revised Edition, published by John Wiley & Sons Canada, Ltd.

THE MARKET COMPARISON APPROACH

This approach is probably the most easily understood concept for a first-time homebuyer or investor. It is also the most commonly used by real estate agents for single-family dwellings. In effect, it is comparison shopping. It involves a comparison of properties similar to the one you are looking at buying. Because no two properties are exactly the same, due to age, location, layout, size, features, upgrades, etc., you will want to obtain comparables that are as close as possible. You will want to have current sale prices.

You may have to make adjustments to the comparable properties to align them as realistic comparisons when you review prices; for example, making price adjustments in the comparison properties for such matters as the circumstances of the sale (e.g., forced sale due to financial problems, order for sale, foreclosure, etc.), special features of the property (e.g., flower garden, arboretum, hot tub, etc.) and location of property (view, privacy, etc.).

The market comparison approach lends itself to situations where there are lots of similar properties and sales. Condominiums, single-family houses, and raw land are the most common types of properties where the market comparison method is applied. Generally, when an appraiser is doing a market comparison appraisal, he compares recent sales of similar properties, similar properties currently "listed" for sale on the market, and properties that did not sell (listings expired). The limitation of the market comparison approach is that similar properties may not be available for comparison at any given time. Also, it is difficult to know the motivations of the vendors of the comparable properties, so in some cases the sale price might not reflect the fair market price.

For example, if you are comparing a condominium for sale against two other identical condominiums in the same complex that have been sold very recently, you will be able to make a fairly close comparison. You could calculate the cost per square foot of the two recent condominium sales and compare with the cost per square foot of the one you are considering. If that latter price is higher, you'll want to know why. Perhaps it has a better view, or is on a higher floor, or the previous owner has made a lot of interior decorating changes to improve the condominium. The point is that the market comparison approach does have its limitations and provides general guidelines only.

THE COST APPROACH

This approach involves calculating the cost to buy a piece of land and build a house, and comparing the cost against existing homes in the area with comparable features. If you calculate that the replacement cost is below market value, you may or may not want to seriously consider the benefits of buying a lot and building on it, in terms of cost savings. That is a separate issue, of course, with its own advantages and disadvantages. There are various steps involved in arriving at a figure using the cost approach.

- **Step I** Estimate the land value, using the market comparison approach discussed earlier. The sale price of similar vacant residential lots in the area should be determined, with adjustments made for such factors as use (zoning), size, location, and features (e.g., view).

- **Step 2** Estimate the cost to construct a new building that is comparable in square footage, features, and quality to the one you are considering. For example, a modest quality construction could be $75 per square foot to replace, whereas a luxury quality construction could be $250 per square foot or more to replace. You will need to obtain comparative and competitive quotes from a contractor.
- **Step 3** If the house you are considering is not new, you would have to calculate a depreciation factor (e.g., reduced value of the building because it is wearing out over time). Calculating the depreciation adjustment factor depends on the building's condition, age, and estimated useful life. Estimated useful life means the point beyond which the building is not economical to repair or maintain. In effect, it would have no market value. If that is the case, you might be buying primarily for lot value and intend to tear down the building or substantially renovate it. A professional appraiser would normally be required to calculate this depreciation factor.
- **Step 4** To determine estimated property value, add the depreciated cost of the building (Steps 2 and 3) to the cost of the land (Step I).

For single-family houses and condominiums, the appraiser normally arrives at an estimate of value as of a certain date by adding the market and cost approach values, and dividing by two. An example of this will be shown below.

EXAMPLE OF ESTIMATE OF MARKET VALUE

Note: This is using only market and cost approaches, which is the normal formula for properties such as houses and condominiums. If you were buying a revenue property (e.g., apartments), you would normally add on the income approach and then take an average of all three approaches.

1. Market Comparison Approach
   Comparison with four similar properties whose prices were $150,000, $155,000, $160,000 and $157,500. Average price is therefore $155,375.
   Market Approach Estimate   **(A) $155,375**

2. Cost Approach
   Land (30 foot x 150 foot lot)
   16,500 square feet @ $5 per square foot $82,500

   Value of improvements on land such as shrubs, trees, fence, garden, tool shed, etc. $7,500

   Construction of building is 1,000 square feet at $75 per square foot construction cost (new) $75,000

   Less 5% depreciation per year because building being purchased is two years old:
   $75,000 − 5% = $71,250 (Year 1), and
   $71,250 − 5% = $67,687.50 (Year 2)

   Therefore, depreciated value of building $67,687.50
   Add value of land + value of improvements + depreciated value of building to arrive at the
   Cost Approach Estimate   **(B) $157,687.50**

FINAL ESTIMATE OF MARKET VALUE
(A + B ÷ 2): $156,531.25

(Market estimate of $155,375, plus cost estimate of $157,687.50, divided by two.)

The limitation of the cost approach is that depreciation might be difficult to correctly estimate. In addition, construction costs vary, depending on location, supply and demand, and inflation. Again, the cost approach value is an estimate only.

> When a professional appraiser writes up a report, the estimate of value is given as an opinion, not a scientific fact. This is helpful to you as a basis for negotiation with the owner. Anyone can have an opinion as to value. The appraisal, though, is only as reliable as the competence, integrity, experience, and objectivity of the appraiser, and the accuracy of information obtained. A real estate appraisal is only as reliable as the assumptions that are made.

• • •

This chapter has covered some of the most common types of techniques for establishing the value of a property purchase for a principal residence property. There are many other formulas that experienced or sophisticated investors may use in addition to the ones noted for investment property.

The important point is to understand the basic concepts and to know when to apply them, to know their limitations, and to use several different formulas to provide some balance when comparing other properties as well as the property itself. The key benefit of these methods is that they can often be quickly calculated to determine if the owner is asking too much, in terms of your purchase criteria, or if the sale is a bargain price. Remember, the rules of thumb are guidelines only.

The calculations could also provide you with negotiating leverage to have the purchase price reduced. You will, of course, want to consider other factors before making your final decision. Also keep in mind that the values are estimates of what that average person would pay. You may not be prepared to pay the estimated price for various reasons, including the following:

- Price is more than you can afford.
- Price is higher than your comfort level in terms of risk.
- Market is starting to decline.
- Overall economic turndown.
- Waiting for more attractive property to invest in.

Conversely, you might be prepared to pay more than the average person. Here are some of the factors that might cause you to consider paying more:

- *New information.* You might be aware of a possible zoning change, subdivision potential, or proposed development nearby.
- *Financing.* You might be able to obtain favourable financial terms (e.g., a low-interest vendor-take-back mortgage or high-ratio financing).
- *Potential for increased income.* The property could have a basement suite.

- *Attractive closing date.* You could get a long closing date, enabling you to get funds that you are expecting from various sources, or to get access to increased mortgage funds by closing, or to sell the agreement of purchase and sale to someone else (almost like having an option).
- *Personal income tax bracket.* Depending on your personal situation, you may be able to offset a negative cash flow against your other income and thus buy a revenue property at a discount price. You would be relying on appreciation and a capital gain in order to change the negative cash flow to a positive one.
- *Required return on your investment.* You might have a lower requirement for your return on your investment than others, if you are buying a revenue property.

Chapter 5

GETTING EXPERT ADVICE BEFORE YOU BUY

When buying real estate, whether you are purchasing a property to live in or as an investment, you need to assemble a team of experts and professionals to assist you in achieving your goals and protecting your interests. This chapter deals with the seven essential experts you need to guide and advise you: realtor, lawyer, accountant, lender, mortgage broker, building inspector, and insurance broker.

QUALITIES TO LOOK FOR IN YOUR REAL ESTATE TEAM

First, be very thorough in your screening process. Choosing the right expert will enhance your prospects for a safe purchase and a property that will increase in value; an unfortunate choice will prove costly in terms of time, money, and stress.

There are many factors you should consider when selecting advisors. For example, professional qualifications, experience in real estate investment, and the fee for services are factors you will want to consider. Prepare a list of questions, plus other items relating to your specific needs, and pose these to each prospective advisor. Some people may feel awkward about discussing fees and qualifications, but it is important to establish these matters at the outset before you make a decision to use a professional's services. The most common selection criteria include qualifications, experience, compatible personality, confidence and competence in the area concerned, and fees. By talking to three professionals in each category, you will be able to make solid comparisons and select the candidates most suited to your needs.

1. QUALIFICATIONS

Before you rely on an advisor or professional, you will want to know that he or she has the appropriate qualifications. These may include a professional degree in the case of a lawyer or accountant, or some other professional training or qualifications relative to the area of work.

2. EXPERIENCE

It is important to assess the advisor's expertise. Such factors as the degree of expertise and experience, and dedication to the respective service are critical factors. For example, the fact that a lawyer might have been practising law for 10 years does not necessarily mean that the lawyer has a high degree of expertise in real estate. Perhaps only 10% of the practice has been spent in that specific area. An accountant with 15 years of experience in small-business accounting and tax advice will certainly provide you with a depth of expertise about small business in general. If that accountant has experience in real estate, this is an additional factor that could assist you. Inquire about the degree of expertise and length of experience in the area that you specifically need. If you don't ask the question, you won't find out the answer that may make the difference between inadequate and in-depth advice.

3. COMPATIBLE PERSONALITY WITH YOUR OWN

When deciding on an advisor, make certain that you feel comfortable with the individual's personality. If you are going to have an ongoing relationship with the advisor, it is important that you feel comfortable with his or her attitude, approach, and commitment to your interests. A healthy respect, candour, and good rapport will put you more at ease when discussing business matters.

4. CONFIDENCE AND COMPETENCE

You must have confidence in your advisor if you are going to rely on their advice to enhance the quality of your decision-making and minimize your risk. After considering the person's qualifications, experience, and personality style, you may feel a strong degree of confidence in the individual. If you do not feel this way, do not choose this person to be an advisor. You will not build trust with this individual.

5. FEES

It is important to feel comfortable with the fees being charged and the payment terms. Are they fair and competitive? Can you afford them? Do they match the person's qualifications and experience? For instance, an experienced real estate lawyer or tax accountant may charge a higher hourly rate than others in their profession, but you may get quality that will save you several thousand dollars. On the other hand, if what you require is the preparation of annual financial statements, perhaps a junior accountant can do the job competently at a more affordable rate. You may want to hire a bookkeeper to do your books, do them yourself, or use one of the many software programs available. Be certain the rate is within your budget, or you may not use the advisor effectively because of the expense. Not using available professional advice when you need it is poor management. Ask at the outset about the estimated fee.

> Do not make a decision about which advisor to use without first checking around. It is a good rule of thumb to see a minimum of three advisors before deciding which is right for you. The more exacting you are in your selection criteria, the more likely that you'll find a good match and the more beneficial that advisor will be to your real estate investment goals. It is a competitive market in the advisory business, and you can afford to be extremely selective when choosing advisors to form your real estate team.

WHEN SELECTING A REALTOR

There are distinct advantages to having a realtor acting for you in buying or selling a property. There are a number of ways to find a qualified and experienced real estate agent:

- Friends, neighbours, and relatives can provide the names of agents with whom they have dealt, and why they would or would not recommend them.
- Open houses provide an opportunity to meet realtors.
- Newspaper ads list the names and phone numbers of agents who are active in your area.
- "For Sale" signs provide an agent's name and phone number.
- Contact real estate firms in your area and speak to an agent who specializes or deals with the type of property you want and is an experienced salesperson.
- Check the Internet for real estate listings and realtors.

After you have met several agents who could potentially meet your needs, there are a number of guidelines to assist you with your selection:

- Favour an agent who is experienced and knowledgeable in the real estate industry.
- Look for an agent who is prepared to pre-screen properties so that you are informed only of those that conform to your guidelines for viewing purposes.
- Look for an agent who is familiar with the various conventional and creative methods of financing, including the effective use of mortgage brokers.
- Look for an agent to be thorough on properties you are keen on, in terms of background information such as length of time on the market, reason for sale, and price comparisons among similar properties. An agent who is familiar with the MLS computer system can find a great deal of information in a short time, assuming the property is listed on the MLS. You can also do your own thorough research of listings on the Internet, using www.mls.ca, and www.google.ca.
- Look for an agent who will be candid with you in suggesting a real estate offer price and explain the reasons for the recommendation.
- Look for an agent who has effective negotiating skills to ensure that your wishes are presented as clearly and persuasively as possible.
- Favour an agent who is working on a full-time basis.
- Look for an agent who is good with numbers; in other words, is familiar with the use of financial calculations. This is particularly important if you are buying revenue (investment) property.

There is an option called a "buyer broker." This is a realtor who will act exclusively on behalf of the buyer. Otherwise, a realtor is considered an agent or sub-agent of the vendor and legally represents the buyer's interests. You will need to sign a contract for a buyer broker. Not all realtors are prepared to act in this capacity, so make enquiries. The buyer broker receives his or her share of the commission from the sale, in the same way that any realtor involved in the sale would receive. You don't pay any commission as the buyer.

> Give the agent your exclusive business if you have confidence in him or her. Keep the agent informed of any open houses in which you are interested. If you are approached by any other agents (who may be hoping to represent you), be sure to advise them that you already have one working for you. Focus clearly on your needs and provide the agent with a written outline of your specific criteria to assist in short-listing potential prospects. If for any reason you are dissatisfied with the agent who is assisting you, find another agent as quickly as possible.

What a Realtor Can Do for a Buyer

One of the key benefits for you as a buyer is that the realtor can act as an intermediary between you and the listing broker. That way, the listing agent cannot exert any influence on you by making a sales pitch, or otherwise make an assessment of you that could compromise your negotiating position. The agent who has the listing agreement with the vendor would only know you through discussions with the realtor you are dealing with and through any offer that you might present. This arm's-length negotiating position is an important strategic tactic that will benefit you in many situations.

In many cases, realtors can refer you to a mortgage broker to assist you in arranging mortgage financing. You still want to get some comparison rates from other mortgage brokers to make sure they are competitive.

WHEN SELECTING A LAWYER

Whether you are the buyer or the seller of real estate, it is essential that you obtain a lawyer to represent your interests—before a purchase and sale takes effect. This is a normal precaution with any real estate transaction. There are many potential legal pitfalls for the unwary when buying real estate. The "agreement for purchase and sale" and related documents are complex. To most people, the purchase of a home or other investment property is the largest financial investment of their lifetime, and the agreement for purchase and sale is the most important legal contract they will ever sign.

There are a number of ways to select the right lawyer for your needs:

- Ask friends who have purchased real estate whom they used, whether they were satisfied with the lawyer, and why.
- Contact the lawyer referral service in your community. Under this service, sponsored by the provincial law society or a provincial division of the Canadian Bar Association, you can consult with a lawyer for a half-hour for either a nominal fee (usually about $25 or slightly more) or for free. Make sure you emphasize that you want a lawyer who specializes in real estate.

- Look in the Yellow Pages under "Lawyers" and check the box ads, which outline the areas of expertise.
- Know the difference between a *notary public* and a *lawyer*. These professional terms are not necessarily interchangeable. In most provinces a lawyer is also automatically a notary public, but a notary public is not necessarily a lawyer. A notary public is not formally trained, qualified, or permitted by law to provide a legal opinion on any subject. He or she can only prepare the required transfer of title documentation, necessary affidavit material, and other related documentary material, and file the documents in the land registry office. In other words, the services provided are primarily technical and procedural. Thus, the buyer or seller of a property is advised to consult a lawyer. In matters relating to properties, you certainly want a legal opinion to avoid the potential risks and pitfalls involved, and to deal with the matter for you if a legal problem arises.

In the province of Quebec, lawyers are referred to as "notaries" (non-courtroom lawyers) or "advocates" (courtroom lawyers). Therefore, in Quebec you would use a "notary" for your property purchase or sale transaction.

Once you have made contact with the lawyer over the phone, enquire as to the areas of his or her real estate interest and expertise. Tell the lawyer that you are looking for a person with expert knowledge in property law. If the lawyer cannot offer this, ask for a recommendation to someone else.

If you did not obtain the referral through a lawyer referral service, ask the lawyer over the phone what a half-hour initial consultation would cost. In many cases it is free, as it is good for the lawyer's business.

Have all your questions and concerns prepared in writing so that you don't forget any. If you wish to make an offer to purchase, bring your offer-to-purchase document with you, and the details about the new, resale, or revenue project you are considering. Ask about anticipated fee and disbursement costs. If you are not pleased with the interview for any reason, see another lawyer.

UNDERSTANDING FEES, DISBURSEMENTS, AND COSTS

In many cases the legal fees will be comparable to what other lawyers are charging. Although competition in the legal profession is obviously a factor in keeping fees comparable, there are many circumstances where two lawyers will charge a different fee for performing the same routine or specialized service.

As in any other business relationship, in order to maintain an effective rapport with your legal advisor, good communication is essential. Be certain that you and your lawyer keep each other informed of matters of importance, so neither is operating without complete information.

If you are in doubt about the particular advice you are being given, you may prefer to get a second opinion. This is reassurance that you are following the best advice for your business. Misunderstandings over fees or other matters should be immediately cleared up to avoid having them mount into serious problems.

If you seriously question a lawyer's invoice, you can have it "taxed" (reviewed) by a court registrar. This is an informal procedure and results in the fee being upheld or reduced. Your local court office will be able to provide further information on the procedure.

WHEN SELECTING AN ACCOUNTANT

If you are buying real estate as an investment, or intend to rent a suite in your home, or operate a business out of your home, you need to get tax advice. An accountant's chief concern is to monitor the financial health of your investment and reduce risks and taxes. Along with your lawyer, your accountant will complement your "real estate team" to ensure that your real estate or business decisions are based on sound advice and good planning.

An accountant can help you right from the pre-purchase phase. The services that can be provided are wide-ranging and include the following:

- Setting up a manual or computerized bookkeeping system that both the investor and accountant can work with efficiently.
- Setting up systems for the control of cash and the handling of funds.
- Preparing or evaluating budgets, forecasts, and investment plans.
- Assessing your break-even point and improving your profitability.
- Preparing and interpreting financial statements.
- Providing tax and financial planning advice.
- Preparing corporate and individual tax returns.

In Canada, anyone can call himself or herself an accountant. One can also adopt the title of "public accountant" without any qualifications, experience, regulations, or accountability to a professional association. That is why you have to be very careful when selecting the appropriate accountant for your needs. There are two main designations of qualified professional accountants in Canada that offer services to the public: Chartered Accountant (CA) and Certified General Accountant (CGA).

Accountants with the above designations are governed by provincial statutes. The conduct, professional standards, training, qualifications, professional development, and discipline of these professionals are regulated by their respective institutes or associations. Rely on the advice of an accountant, therefore, only after you have satisfied yourself that the accountant meets the professional qualifications that you require for your real estate investment needs.

> For further information, contact the professional institute or association for the specific accounting designation and ask for information. You can obtain the contact phone number from the Yellow Pages under "Accountants," from the Internet, or through the Helpful Websites section in the Appendix of this book. The governing bodies are referred to as the Institute of Chartered Accountants, and the Certified General Accountants' Association.

How to Find an Accountant

- *Referral by business associates, banker, or lawyer.* Often a banker, lawyer, or other business associate will be pleased to recommend an accountant. Such referrals are valuable since these individuals are probably aware of your area of interest and would recommend an accountant only if they felt he or she was well qualified and had a good track record.
- *Professional associations.* The professional institute that governs CAs and CGAs may be a source of leads. You can

telephone or email the institute or association with a request for the names of three accountants who provide public accounting services in your area. It is not uncommon for an initial consultation to be free of charge, for marketing and client acquisition purposes. Ask in advance.

- *The Yellow Pages.* In the Yellow Pages, under the heading "Accountants," you will find listings under the categories "Chartered," and "Registered." Also check out the Internet, and the list of associations under Helpful Websites.

Prior to a meeting with your accountant, make a list of your questions and concerns. As noted earlier, you will want to know the person's qualifications, areas of expertise, and method of record keeping you would require (e.g., is a computerized system used or necessary for your needs?). Ask the accountant what his or her range of experience is in your type of investment: tax, business management advice, accessing financing, etc. Ask about fees, how they are determined, how accounts are rendered, and what retainer may be required. Ask who will be working on your file: the accountant, junior accountant, or a bookkeeper? It is common for accountants to delegate routine work to junior staff and keep the more intricate matters for their own review.

Understanding Fees and Costs

Accountants' fees vary according to experience, specialty, type of service provided, size of firm, and other considerations. They can range from $40 per hour for basic bookkeeping, to $150 or more per hour for tax or accounting advice. It is common for an accountant to have different charge-out rates for the various activities performed: bookkeeping, preparation of financial statements, tax consultation, and advice. For example, if an accountant is doing bookkeeping, it will be at a lower rate scale; complex tax advice is charged at the high end of the range. Accountants generally charge for their time plus additional costs such as bookkeeper, secretary, etc. The bill-out rates for these staff members do vary and you should ask exactly what you will be charged in advance.

As with your lawyer, a good level of rapport and communication with your accountant will enhance the quality of advice and the effectiveness of your use of that advice. Openly discuss your concerns and questions with your accountant. If you are not satisfied with your accountant for any reason, you should find another accountant who may better meet your needs.

WHEN SELECTING A LENDER

When selecting a bank, credit union, or other financial institution to deal with for your mortgage needs, it is advisable to shop around for the best service and rates. You will even find that service, attitude, and mortgage-financing flexibility can vary among branches of the same lending institution. You also need to use the services of a mortgage broker, which is covered next. More information on dealing with lenders is covered in Part II.

WHEN SELECTING A MORTGAGE BROKER

The mortgage financing business has become very complicated as rates, terms, and conditions constantly change. Each lending institution has its own criteria that apply to potential borrowers. Some insist on a particular type of property as security, while others require a certain type of applicant. In this latter case, factors such as type of employment, job stability, income, and credit background are weighed. There is a broad range of policies lending institutions apply to an applicant's qualifications.

Mortgage brokers make it their business to know lenders' plans and lending policies, as well as their policies on mortgage security and covenants. They also know what incentive deals any particular lender might have at any given time (e.g., free legal fees up to $500, including the appraisal fee). A mortgage broker is in effect a matchmaker who introduces the appropriate lender to the (hopefully) qualified purchaser. The broker receives a commission from the lender.

Mortgage brokers have access to numerous sources of funds, including the following:

- conventional lenders such as banks and credit unions
- Canada Mortgage and Housing Corporation (CMHC)
- private pension funds
- union pension funds
- real estate syndication funds
- foreign bank subsidiaries
- insurance companies
- private lenders

THE TYPES OF MORTGAGE BROKERS

I. *Traditional mortgage broker.* This is an independent mortgage broker, normally working from one location, who represents a wide variety of institutional, syndicated, and private lenders.

    The normal procedure is for you to complete an application form supplied by the mortgage broker, provide a copy of the agreement of purchase and sale, as well as provide proof of employment, length of time employed, and annual salary. A letter from your employer is frequently required. If you are self-employed, you are normally required to provide the last three years of financial statements of your business and/or copies of the last three income tax returns for your business.

You pay the mortgage broker the cost of obtaining an appraisal of your property. (This cost may be reimbursed by the lender.) The broker also does a credit bureau search. The broker then attempts to find a lender who will lend you money based on your financial needs, the terms you require, and the information that you have supplied.

2. *Franchise/chain-type mortgage broker.* This type of broker is usually associated with a chain of representatives/offices across the country that are company-owned, or alternatively is an independent broker licensed to represent the company.

   The company arranges with a number of financial institutions, both national and local, to "bid" on your request for mortgage financing. The broker has you complete an application form and provide a copy of the agreement of purchase and sale; he then packages a summary of the other information you have supplied, along with the appraisal and credit bureau report, and forwards it to the lenders who are associated with the company "mortgage lender program." The lenders normally have a one- or two-day deadline in which to reply. You are then given a summary of the lenders who are prepared to finance you, along with the amount, terms, and conditions.

3. *Online mortgage application.* Almost all mortgage brokers noted above have their own websites, and most of the applications are done online. You can also apply online for mortgages by companies that operate online only. You will receive competitive rates to consider. To obtain websites for online mortgage companies, do a search on www.google.ca with keywords such as "Canadian mortgages online" and other variations.

What Services Do Mortgage Brokers Offer?

1. They arrange a simple mortgage that will generally get automatic approval in your particular circumstance. As a consequence, this saves you a lot of time searching for a lender and a mortgage. As mentioned, the broker generally receives a commission directly from the lender, as a "finder" or "referral" fee. You don't pay any extra money or higher interest. Lenders do this because the mortgage market is so competitive.

2. They can arrange for a more complex mortgage that may not be automatically approved by a lender. This takes more time, skill, and persuasion on the part of the broker to source a lender or number of lenders who will provide the funds you need. For example, if you do not have a sufficient down payment, have a poor credit rating, are highly leveraged already as a real estate investor, have been self-employed for a short time, or do not have the level of income required, you will probably be turned down by a conventional lender such as a bank or credit union.

If a mortgage broker succeeds in arranging your financing, given the types of challenging factors noted above, you would pay a commission. The commission could be between 1% and 5% of the amount of the mortgage arranged, depending on the time the broker requires to source funds and the degree of urgency. In some provinces there is legislation that prohibits a mortgage broker from charging an advance fee (application fee) if the mortgage amount is below a certain level. Mortgage brokers are regulated by provincial legislation.

In addition, mortgage brokers place private financing for people who want to lend money out with mortgages as security, or buy existing private mortgages at a discount. This topic is covered in more detail in Part II.

To find a mortgage broker, look in the Yellow Pages of your telephone directory, check the Internet, or ask your real estate lawyer or your realtor. Refer to the Helpful Websites section in the Appendix for the Canadian Institute of Mortgage Brokers and Lenders, for contact brokers in each province. Remember to comparison shop by having at least three competitive mortgage broker quotes before deciding upon with whom to deal.

WHEN SELECTING A HOME INSPECTOR

One of the most important aspects of purchasing your principal residence or investment property is to know the condition of the property in advance. You don't want to be saddled with expensive repairs after you buy.

It is therefore a wise step to have a professional building inspector examine the building and give you a written opinion as to its condition and the approximate range of costs to repair the problems. The older the building, the more potential there is for problems, but new buildings can have serious problems as well. Building inspectors look at all the key components and systems of the building, such as the roof, siding, foundation, basement, flooring, walls, drainage, electrical, heating, plumbing, and so on. Among other things they look for are wood rot, mould, and insects. Building inspection fees range from approximately $200 to $400 and more, depending on the expertise and nature of inspection. Put a condition in your agreement of purchase and sale offer that says "subject to purchaser obtaining a building inspection satisfactory to the purchaser within X days of acceptance of the offer."

Make sure that the inspector is qualified and comes with references. Avoid a contractor who may hope to get the repair business from you. Look in the Yellow Pages of your telephone directory under "Building Inspection Services" and on the Internet. Refer to the Helpful Websites section in the Appendix for the website of the Canadian Association of Home and Property Inspectors.

WHEN SELECTING AN INSURANCE BROKER

A broker is not committed to any particular insurance company and therefore can compare and contrast the different policies, coverage, and premiums from a wide range of companies that relate to the type of insurance coverage that you are looking for.

Also, insurance brokers can obtain a premium quotation for you and coverage availability from insurance company underwriters if the particular investment you have is unique or difficult to cover by typical existing policies.

Insurance brokers generally have a wide range of types of insurance available to the customer. It is important to have confidence in the broker in terms of his or her expertise, qualifications, and experience.

Every real estate building needs insurance. Insurance is frequently required by creditors, such as a mortgage lender. Ask the insurance broker for brochures describing the main types of insurance and an explanation of each, or check online information by going to www.google.ca. The three main categories and types of insurance that you should consider and discuss with your insurance broker are mentioned below. There are many other types as well, including home office insurance, personal liability protection insurance, rental loss insurance, etc.

1. *Property insurance.* Property insurance covers destruction or damage to the insured property caused by a certain peril specified in the coverage, such as fire, flood, and burglary. You want to make sure to obtain replacement coverage. Property insurance also covers property items such as glass (from breakage) and automobiles (from collision, theft, fire, and vandalism).

2. *Liability insurance.* Liability insurance covers any area in which the business (for example, a home-based business) or the owners, employees, or agents who might be held liable for negligence, or some other act or omission. The most common type of liability insurance is general liability, which

covers negligence causing injury to tenants, guests, and the general public. For example, if you invited guests over for dinner and a guest tripped on your carpet and was seriously injured, or someone slipped on your driveway and injured themselves, you could be sued.

3. *Life insurance.* Life insurance obviously covers the life of the individual. There are various forms of life insurance used by those buying real estate, including whole life, term life, and bank loan or mortgage insurance.

> You can find an insurance broker by looking in the Yellow Pages under "Insurance Brokers" or on the Internet. You can also obtain names of brokers from friends, business associates or your accountant or lawyer. Refer to the Helpful Websites section in the Appendix. Remember, whenever you are selecting professional real estate or business advisors, speak to at least three advisors in each area. This will provide you with an objective basis for comparison and selection.

Part II

ALL ABOUT MORTGAGES

Chapter 6

Mortgage Basics

If you have been considering the purchase of a house, condominium, or real estate investment for some time, you probably have some savings already set aside for a down payment. You also might have some idea of how large a mortgage you need for the property you want. But it all boils down to how much a lending institution deems you can afford to borrow.

This chapter covers what a mortgage is, the different types of mortgages, and the sources of mortgage financing. A term you should be familiar with is "equity," which is the difference between the amount for which the property could be sold and what you still owe on your mortgage.

WHAT IS A MORTGAGE?

A mortgage is a contract between one party who wants to borrow money and another party who wants to lend money. The borrower is referred to as the "mortgagor" and the lender is referred to as the "mortgagee." These terms can sometimes be confusing. The terms "borrower" and "lender" are also used.

The mortgage agreement states that in exchange for the money that the lender is providing, the borrower will provide security to the lender in the form of a mortgage document to be filed against the property. For the purposes of this book, the term "property" will refer to the purchase you are considering, whether it be a condominium, house, multi-dwelling (such as duplex, fourplex, apartment), or raw land. The mortgage document specifies the rights that the lender has to the property in the event the borrower stops making mortgage payments.

A mortgage document filed against the title of the property in a provincial land registry office provides security to the mortgagee against other creditors that the mortgagor may have. If a first mortgage is filed against the property and there are no other encumbrances or charges against the property, then the amount outstanding on the first mortgage takes priority over any and all other creditors (i.e., in the event of default, it is paid off first from the sale of the property). Additional loans could be obtained by the mortgagor, which would mean that additional mortgages are filed against the property; a second or third or fourth mortgage could be filed against the property. Each mortgage ranks lower in priority than the previous, as the date of registration is the criterion that determines priority.

Because of the increasing risk involved for subsequent mortgages, higher interest rates are charged. For example, the first mortgage interest rate may be 6%; the second 10%; the third 16%; and the fourth 20%. The first mortgage would be paid out in full from any proceeds of sale, followed by the second mortgage, and so on. It is possible that the price for which a home would sell may only cover the payout on the first and second mortgages in this example, leaving no funds available to pay out the third and fourth. This could be the case especially if the real estate market undergoes a significant downturn.

Mortgages are regulated by federal and provincial law. Although the laws may be different from one province to another, the description of a mortgage outlined in this book applies to most mortgages. The method of mortgage registration and the enforcement laws are the main areas of variation between provinces.

TITLE INSURANCE

Many lenders and borrowers are now taking out title insurance. This type of insurance protects you in case there are any "defects" in the title of the property, such as charges or claims that have not been filed on the property title, or that were filed but not picked up on the searches before ownership passed to you. For example, maybe a survey was not done, or it was an old property survey, and the boundaries of your property are not what you thought you were getting. Title insurance could also cover you for mortgages that were discharged and paid out, but still remain on title, and certain construction liens.

Another benefit of title insurance is to protect you from title fraud. Here are some examples:

- Someone fraudulently refinances your property by forging your signature and using fake identification, obtains the funds, and cannot be found. You are left to defend your title and pay all the legal costs.
- Someone fraudulently transfers the title of your property out of your name, by forging your signature and using fake identification. They then obtain a mortgage or several mortgages on the property without your knowledge, and cannot be found. You are left with the responsibility of paying the mortgage and reclaiming your property ownership.

You can imagine the prolonged stress, uncertainty, negative energy and time, and financial legal costs of trying to protect your property rights and dealing with the financial fraud. If you had the right type of title insurance, you would have peace of mind. The insurance covers you from the time you take title until you sell your home. Title insurance will cover you for your legal fees to defend your right of ownership, which could cost tens of thousands of dollars, as well as your actual financial losses. You can see why so many Canadian homeowners want to have the protection of title insurance.

TYPES OF MORTGAGES

Mortgages are available from banks, credit unions, mortgage companies, private lenders, and the government. Even the person from whom you are buying the property may offer financing (known as a vendor-back or vendor-take-back mortgage). Although most residential property borrowers obtain financing through a conventional mortgage, it is wise to be aware of other alternatives. Here is a brief discussion of the main types of mortgages.

CONVENTIONAL MORTGAGE

The conventional mortgage is the most common type of financing for a principal residence or residential investment property. It is fairly standard in its terms and conditions, although there can be variations. In this type of mortgage, the loan generally cannot exceed 75% of the appraised value or purchase price of the property, whichever is the lesser of the two. The purchaser is responsible for raising the other 25% of the funds necessary, either through a down payment or through other means, such as a second mortgage or vendor-take-back mortgage.

Most financial institutions, including banks and credit unions, offer conventional mortgages. In most cases these mortgages do not have to be insured, but occasionally a lender may require it. For example, if the building is older or is smaller than is normally required by the policy of the lender, or if it is located in a rural or rundown area, then the mortgage may be required to be insured with the Canada Mortgage and Housing Corporation (CMHC) or Genworth Financial. CMHC is a federal Crown corporation, and Genworth is the largest private insurer in Canada.

A conventional mortgage is normally a fixed-interest rate mortgage or a variable-rate mortgage. A fixed-rate mortgage means a mortgage that has a fixed interest rate and fixed payments for the term of the mortgage. The mortgage term is normally 1, 3, 5, 7, or 10 years before it has to be renewed. The payments are calculated based on an amortization period (to clear the mortgage in full) of usually 15, 20, 25, or 30 years, and based on the frequency of payment (e.g., weekly, bi-weekly, monthly, etc.).

A variable-rate mortgage is quite a different format. This type of mortgage, sometimes referred to as a VRM, is quite different from a fixed-interest and fixed-payment mortgage, as the interest rate charged on the mortgage may be changed during the term of the mortgage. Generally, these mortgages are initially set up like a fixed mortgage, based on the current interest rate. The mortgage is reviewed at specific intervals, such as once a month. Some lenders adjust it monthly or quarterly. If the market mortgage or prime interest rate changes, the interest charged on the mortgage changes. The mortgage repayment formula is usually altered by changing either the size of the monthly payments or the length of the amortization period, or both.

When interest rates are stable or going down, a VRM is a popular option. The object is to attempt to project the mortgage interest-rate trend and financially benefit by decreasing rates. On the other hand, if interest rates are going up, there is no incentive to have a VRM. At that point, many people choose to convert the VRM into an open or closed mortgage. The lending institution normally charges a modest "conversion" fee.

Some people prefer to have a variable rate mortgage, as the savings on the interest-rate spread could range from 1% to 2% compared to a fixed-term mortgage. You must monitor the money market for interest-rate changes so that you can convert quickly if there is an indication that interest rates are going up. Others prefer to lock in a fixed-term rate for five, seven, or 10 years if the interest rate is low, so that they can budget accordingly, and do not have to be concerned about volatile mortgage rates.

Another reason to effect a change to a fixed rate, in the above example, is the risk of negative or reverse amortization. If your current VRM mortgage includes a potential for negative amortization, that alone may be a strong argument in favour of refinancing. As you may know, amortization is the process by which you gradually pay off the principal amount of your mortgage loan. Negative amortization is what happens when the process goes into reverse. If your monthly payments are "capped" or "fixed" at a level where the effective interest charges on your mortgage are not being covered, the lender may have the right to add the shortfall to the principal amount of your mortgage. In other words, while you are making what may appear to be attractive monthly payments, you are actually accumulating more debt and paying interest on that extra debt.

For the above reason, in terms of potential risk, most lenders will not approve a loan-to-value ratio of more than 70% for a conventional VRM mortgage, to allow for a buffer of 5% relative to the conventional 75% loan-to-value ratio for a fixed-interest rate mortgage. This difference of 5% allows for the potential risk of negative amortization.

High-Ratio Insured Mortgage

If you are unable to raise a 25% down payment to take out a conventional mortgage, a high-ratio mortgage may be available to you. These mortgages are required to be insured, if issued by a bank or credit union, and in excess of 75% financing, and they are available only through approved lenders, through CMHC or Genworth, unless the lender self-insures the amount. For example, some credit unions will do that. They will lend up to 80% financing and charge a high-ratio insurance fee on the total mortgage amount. This fee might be 0.25% less, for example, than the equivalent CMHC premium, as it is administratively less time-consuming for the credit union to process.

Both CMHC and Genworth have specific guidelines for a borrower to qualify for a high-ratio mortgage, but the administration is primarily done through the bank, trust company, or credit union. The purpose of the insurance is to protect and, if required, pay the lender in the event of a mortgage default and eventual shortfall of funds to pay the mortgage on sale of the property.

High-ratio mortgages are available for up to 90% of the purchase price or of the appraisal, whichever is lower, and in some cases 95%. There is a premium for this insurance, generally between 0.5% and 3% of the amount of the mortgage. The amount of premium is related to risk. The higher the debt ratio, the higher the risk, and therefore the higher the premium. The high-ratio percentage for which you would be eligible depends on various circumstances, for example, if the purchase is for a principal residence or real estate investment. There are also restrictions on the purchase price of the home that may be involved, as well as other conditions. Obtain more information from your realtor, banker, mortgage broker, or Genworth or CMHC directly.

GOVERNMENT-ASSISTED MORTGAGES

National Housing Act (NHA) mortgages are loans granted under the provisions of this federal act. They are administered through CMHC. You can apply for an NHA loan at any chartered bank, trust company, or credit union. Borrowers must pay an application fee to CMHC that usually includes the cost of a property appraisal and an insurance fee. The latter is usually added to the principal amount of the mortgage, though it may be paid at the time of closing. Contact CMHC or your financial institution for the most current information on borrowing requirements.

In addition, some provinces have second mortgage funding or funding guarantees available for principal residence home purchases. Generally there is a limit on the amount of the purchase price of the home, and a ceiling on the amount of the mortgage. Obtain further information from your realtor or lending institution. For other government incentive or assistance programs, refer to Chapter 10.

COLLATERAL MORTGAGE

In a collateral mortgage, the mortgage security is secondary, or collateral, to some other main form of security taken by the lender. This main security may take the form of a promissory note, personal guarantee, or assignment of some other form of security that the lender may require. A collateral mortgage is, then, a form of insurance or protection for the loan that is filed against the property. The payment requirements on the loan are covered in the promissory note, and once the promissory note has been paid off in full, the collateral mortgage will automatically be paid off. You would then be entitled to have the collateral mortgage discharged from the title of the property.

One of the main differences between a collateral mortgage and a conventional mortgage is that a conventional mortgage may be assumed, whereas a collateral mortgage, of course, cannot be, as it is subject to some other form of security between the parties. Otherwise, the terms of the collateral mortgage could be very similar to the terms of a conventional mortgage. The money borrowed on a collateral mortgage could be used for the purchase of the property itself, or for other purposes such as home improvements or other real estate investments.

SECONDARY FINANCING

Secondary financing generally means that a second mortgage, or possibly a third, is taken out against the property. Let's say you are assuming a first mortgage on the property you're buying, and that it has an attractive interest rate. But the mortgage isn't large enough. So you'll take out a second mortgage to make up the difference between the purchase price and your down payment plus the first mortgage.

Chartered banks will usually provide money for second mortgages up to a limit of 75% of the lesser of the purchase price or appraised value. You can also obtain second mortgages through mortgage brokers or other sources that could go up as high as 90% of the lesser of the purchase price or appraised value.

If the second mortgage has a term that is longer than that of the first mortgage you assume, make sure that you have a postponement clause put into the second mortgage. With this clause you would be able to automatically renew or replace the first mortgage when it becomes due without having to obtain the permission from the second mortgage lender to do so. In other words, if you renewed the mortgage or obtained a replacement first mortgage, that mortgage would still be in first position, ahead of the second mortgage. Your lawyer will advise you.

WRAP-AROUND MORTGAGE

In a situation where a property owner requires additional financing, and there is already a first mortgage on the property, the owner has some options. If the first mortgage has an open term, it can be paid out without penalty, and a new, larger first mortgage would be filed in the land registry office to replace it. Alternatively, a conventional second mortgage could be arranged to raise the money needed and the existing first mortgage would remain in place.

Another alternative is a second mortgage called a wrap-around mortgage. Here is how a wrap-around mortgage works. The borrower signs the document and the wrap-around mortgage is filed in the land registry office and will show up as a second mortgage. Under the terms of the mortgage, the borrower makes only one payment to the wrap-around lender. The wrap-around lender keeps his part of the payment for funds advanced, and forwards the required first mortgage payment to the first mortgage lender. There is less risk of the first mortgage payments being late, as the wrap-around lender controls the first mortgage payments. Because of this lower risk, the wrap-around lender charges a lower interest rate on the additional funds provided by the wrap-around mortgage than would a conventional second mortgage lender.

ASSUMED MORTGAGE

In the case of an assumed mortgage, you are qualified by the lender to assume an existing mortgage on the property. In some instances mortgages can be assumed without requiring you to qualify. If you assume the existing mortgage, it will save you the cost of legal fees and disbursements for registering the mortgage, obtaining an appraisal, and other expenses. Whenever you are assuming an existing mortgage, it is important that your lawyer obtain for you a mortgage assumption statement showing the principal balance outstanding, the method of paying taxes, the remaining term on the mortgage, and a copy of the mortgage that shows other features such as prepayment privileges, etc.

CONSTRUCTION MORTGAGE

If you are building the house, the lender may approve a mortgage for construction purposes but will advance mortgage draws based on the various stages of construction (e.g., foundation, framing, roofing, etc.). There could be three or more stages. It depends on the nature of the construction and the policy of the lender.

DISCOUNTED MORTGAGE FROM A BUILDER

Another variation is that a builder will offer you a discounted mortgage. In other words, to make the house price attractive, the builder offers a 4% mortgage rate at a time when conventional rates are 6%. The builder is able to "buy down" a mortgage from a lender at an attractive rate by paying a discount; in other words, the difference in financial terms between what the lender would make on a 4% mortgage and what he would make on a 6% mortgage. However, the builder will frequently add the difference to the purchase price of the home: you pay a lower interest rate but a higher than normal purchase price. Another factor to be aware of is that the discounted mortgage may have a very short term, such as a year, and after that you will have to obtain your own mortgage at the going rate. Thus, although a discounted mortgage could initially appear attractive, over the long term it could be false economy. Check the figures carefully.

VENDOR-BACK MORTGAGE

A vendor mortgage is sometimes referred to as a vendor-back or vendor-take-back mortgage. Here, the vendor encourages the sale of the property by providing a loan to the purchaser of the property. For example, if the purchaser is able to get 75% conventional financing but does not have sufficient funds for a down payment of 25%, the vendor may be prepared to give, in effect, a second mortgage for 15% of the purchase price. That way, the purchaser would only need to come up with a 10% down payment. The purchaser would then make mortgage payments to the vendor as if a normal commercial lender held the second mortgage.

If you are the purchaser, it is fairly common for the vendor not to make any credit check or any other financial assessment of you. On the other hand, if you are the vendor, for obvious reasons you should make sure that there is a provision in the offer to purchase that you can do a thorough credit check of the purchaser before deciding to grant the second mortgage.

Sometimes the vendor makes arrangements through a mortgage broker for the second mortgage to be sold at a discount as soon as the transaction is completed. This way, the vendor gets cash immediately, minus, of course, the cost required to discount the mortgage and the broker's fee. (For more discussion on calculating a discounted mortgage, refer to the chapter on investing in mortgages.) Generally, the following is true of a vendor-takeback mortgage: it has to have a fixed and not a variable rate if it is to be sold; the terms should be at least a year to be attractive to a purchaser of the mortgage; the mortgage is generally closed with a penalty for early payment; and the mortgage is generally not assumable.

Equity Mortgage

If you have equity in your home (that is, the net amount left after deducting the debt (mortgage) from the value of the home), you can normally raise money. Lenders will generally lend up to 75%

of the equity of the home, depending on your ability to make the monthly payments, the reason for the loan, and the state of the real estate market. For example, if the real estate market is falling, the lender, to avoid risk, might only lend 60% or 50% of the equity.

The format for the mortgage which is registered in the land registry office is normally in the form of a second mortgage, or a collateral mortgage to a demand loan, depending on how you originally structured the deal. The full amount of funds could be given to you at once or in the form of a line of credit. In this latter case you may not need to use all the funds right away and may want to repay the funds used from time to time, thereby saving on interest. The line of credit gives you the right to borrow up to the stated limit at any time.

The interest rate for an equity mortgage is normally a variable rate of 0.5% to 1% or more above the lending rate of the lender. Prime rate, as you know, is the rate lenders charge to their most creditworthy customers. Some lenders require you to pay only the interest every month, while others require you to also make a payment to reduce the principal.

If you are using the equity mortgage to buy revenue or investment property or to invest in a business, the interest is deductible. There could be situations where you would prefer to have a "standard" second mortgage with a fixed term, an amortization period, a fixed interest rate, and a fixed payment schedule. Obtain tax and legal advice. You would pay legal and associated costs for the mortgage preparation and registration, as with any mortgage.

If you just want a small line of credit and own a home, many lenders will lend you up to $5,000 or $10,000 without requiring you to incur the cost of having a mortgage prepared and registered. Lenders' policies vary, so check and compare.

BLANKET MORTGAGE

A blanket mortgage, sometimes called an "inter-alia" mortgage, is a mortgage registered over two or more properties. The purpose is to provide the lender with additional property as security. It is normally used where a borrower wants more money than the lender is prepared to provide on the basis of one property alone. That property may not have sufficient equity and, for example, the amount of money that is being requested could constitute 90% or 95% of the value of the first property. If the second property has attractive equity, the lender may be prepared to advance the funds to the borrower, but have one mortgage filed against both properties. In the event of default, the lender could proceed against one or both of the properties in order to get sufficient proceeds from sale to satisfy the outstanding debt.

NON-RECOURSE MORTGAGE

This is not a common type of mortgage in Canada for residential mortgages. It means that if the borrower breaches the mortgage terms and the lender has to take legal action to protect its security, the lender can only claim against the property to offset the mortgage debt owing. The lender has no recourse or claim against the borrower *personally* for the debt or any shortfall on the debt.

The term is more common in the United States. For example, a Canadian buying a property in the U.S. to reside in for six months a year, may wish to minimize U.S. tax on the sale of the property by negotiating with a lender for a non-recourse mortgage. In that way, the tax would be based on the equity only, not the full amount of the sale price of the dwelling, which would normally be the case if it was a "recourse" mortgage. There is generally an exemption for a certain amount of otherwise taxable income on the sale of a property in the U.S. If you are buying in the U.S., obtain advice from a professional accountant. A U.S. lender might be agreeable to a non-recourse mortgage if it believes there is sufficient equity in the property.

Normally in Canada, mortgages are automatically "recourse" mortgages. In other words, the lender has recourse against the borrower personally for the debt and/or any shortfall on the sale of the property.

LEASEHOLD MORTGAGES

A leasehold mortgage is a mortgage on a house, condominium, or other property in which the land is leased rather than owned. The mortgage must be amortized over a period that is shorter than the length of the land lease. Usually a lender will not grant a mortgage on leasehold property unless the duration of the lease is of sufficient length that the risk is fairly minimal to the lender. For example, if a condominium is on leasehold land with a 99-year lease and there are 85 years left on the lease, then there is relatively little risk to the lender for advancing funds with, say, a five-year term. On the other hand, if the leasehold is for a 30-year period and there are only five years left on the lease, the lender will consider the risk too high, because at the end of the five-year period the lease will expire and therefore there is no right or entitlement to the leasehold interest. This would mean that the condominium would have no value to a potential purchaser after five years in the above example. The main lease would revert back to the lessor (i.e., the original owner of the land).

CONDOMINIUM MORTGAGE

In many cases condominium mortgages are identical to any of the other mortgages discussed in terms of the provisions, except for a few special provisions because of the unique nature of a condominium. Although a purchaser of a condominium receives a legal title to one individual unit, the purchaser also has an undivided interest in the common elements of the development.

Some of the special clauses contained in most condominium mortgages that distinguish this type of mortgage from a conventional house mortgage are as follows:

1. The lender has the right to use the unit owner's vote or consent in the condominium corporation. In other words, the lender has a proxy to vote in place of the borrower. In practical terms, the lender does not usually vote on any and all decisions in normal circumstances. The lender, though, can require that the borrower provide notice of all condominium corporation meetings, including special or extraordinary meetings announced by the condominium corporation, and copies of minutes and information.

2. The lender requires that the borrower comply with all the terms of the bylaws, rules, and regulations of the condominium corporation. Any default on the borrower's part will constitute default under the mortgage.

3. The lender requires the borrower to pay the appropriate portion of maintenance costs of the common elements. In the event of failure of the borrower to do so, the lender is entitled to pay the costs on behalf of the borrower and add these onto the principal amount outstanding on the mortgage, with interest charged to this amount.

Agreement for Sale

An agreement for sale is not actually a mortgage, but it is another way of financing a sale. It should not be confused with an agreement for purchase and sale. An agreement for sale is normally used in a situation where the buyer of the property does not have sufficient funds for a down payment and the vendor wishes to dispose of the property.

In an agreement for sale, the vendor finances the purchase of the property in a fashion similar to that of a vendor-takeback mortgage. The purchaser, though, does not become the legal owner of the property until the agreement for sale has been paid in full. At that time, the purchaser is legally entitled to have the conveyance of the legal interest of the property transferred over to the purchaser. In the meantime, the vendor remains the registered owner on title of the property. The purchaser has the legal right of possession and makes regular payments to the vendor under the terms of the agreement between the vendor and the purchaser. The purchaser's legal "right to purchase" is registered against the title of the property in the provincial land registry office.

The terms of an agreement for sale are in many ways very similar to the terms found in a mortgage. The agreement for sale may be amortized over 25 years and have a five-year term, for example, after which time the full amount is due and payable. At that time either the purchaser has to arrange conventional mortgage financing or other form of financing to pay off the vendor, or else make an agreement with the vendor for an extension of the agreement for sale for another term. Agreements for sale are frequently used where the purchaser cannot qualify to assume the existing mortgage or to obtain a new mortgage; in effect, the purchaser assumes a mortgage that would otherwise be unassumable. The purchaser pays the vendor and the vendor maintains payments on the underlying mortgage.

SOURCES OF MORTGAGE FUNDS

It is important to keep in mind that the competition among institutions to provide mortgage financing is extremely intense. There are numerous lenders of mortgage funds and they are all attempting to attract the customer to use their services. You should therefore do thorough research before deciding on which mortgage lender to use.

In today's market, consumers are getting more street-smart about mortgage rates. They realize they can ask for and expect to get a mortgage "wholesale" (that is, at a discounted rate) rather than "retail" (that is, the "posted" or published rate). You can make a comparison of mortgage interest rates by checking the financial section of your newspaper or online.

The main sources of mortgage funds available for residential or investment purchases that you may wish to consider, are as follows:

- Commercial banks.
- Government. As mentioned earlier, the federal government, through CMHC, provides mortgage funds if you qualify. In addition, many provincial governments have second mortgage funding or mortgage guarantees available; again, if you qualify.
- Through a vendor-back or vendor-take-back mortgage.
- Assuming an existing mortgage.
- Obtaining funds from personal sources such as family, relatives, friends, or business associates.
- Mortgage companies. Check in the Yellow Pages under "Mortgages" and the Internet for online mortgages.
- Real estate companies. Many real estate companies that are associated with trust companies have protocol established

for pre-approved mortgages. Because of the natural vested interest in terms of the connection between the real estate firm and the trust company, this can sometimes facilitate a more flexible gross debt service ceiling criterion in order for the sale to complete. Of course, the usual financial qualification criteria for creditworthiness would apply.

- Mortgage brokers.

> Keep in mind that most lenders have lots of money in the till after RRSP season. They want to get it out in the form of mortgages to start earning money on those customer RRSP deposits. So, they tend to offer lots of competitive incentive packages to compete with the marketplace.

HOW MUCH MORTGAGE CAN YOU SAFELY CARRY?

Different lenders have different criteria for approving the amount of mortgage funds they will advance to you. You must compare lenders or have a mortgage broker do so on your behalf in order to get the money, terms, and rate you're looking for. Lenders use the Gross Debt Service Ratio and Total Debt Service Ratio as standard formulas for determining mortgage qualification. There are other forms of calculations that you may want to utilize that would be helpful to you in determining the data relating to mortgages.

In calculating principal and interest and other factors such as payment frequency, you can do it the old "delayed gratification" way by using an amortization table or mortgage interest booklet, and doing the math. The more expedient way is go on the Internet and get instant gratification. Go to www.google. ca and type in keywords such as "mortgage calculator Canada." Another source is at www.cmhc.ca. These mortgage calculator sites will help you determine how much mortgage money can be made available to you.

The examples below simply describe the process that lenders go through.

Gross Debt Service (GDS) Ratio

The GDS Ratio is used to calculate the amount you can afford to spend for mortgage principal (P) and interest (I) payments. Some lenders also include property taxes (T) as part of this formula, and possibly heating costs (H) as well. All of these expenses are added together. Under the GDS Ratio, payments generally should not exceed 30% of your income. There is flexibility in lending criteria, though, as some lenders will go up to 32% and in some cases 35% or more of your income and only include P and I rather than PIT or PITH. (Refer to Sample Form #3 in the Appendix to calculate your own mortgage eligibility.) If you have no additional monthly debt obligations, as discussed in determining the Total Debt Service Ratio (described next), some lenders will go as high as 40% for the GDS ratio. If you deal through a mortgage broker, they know which lenders are more flexible in terms of GDS ceilings.

Some lenders will take into account any rental income you receive for renting out part of your home (sometimes called a "mortgage helper") and add the rental income onto the amount previously calculated for annual GDS to determine the amount of mortgage that you are eligible for. This would entitle you to a larger mortgage than if the lender added the rental income onto your gross income and then calculated the GDS. The formula used depends on the lender's policy and how it views your debt-servicing capacity and other related risk factors (e.g., high vacancy rates in the community at that point in time).

High-ratio mortgage insurance companies such as CMHC and Genworth generally permit utilizing income from a suite in a principal residence home for the purpose of approving mortgage amount eligibility for a high-ratio CMHC-insured mortgage.

Total Debt Service (TDS) Ratio

Many people have monthly financial obligations other than mortgage and taxes, and lenders want to know what these are in order to determine ability to debt service the mortgage. Using the TDS Ratio, the lender would want to know your fixed monthly debts such as credit-card payments, car payments, other loans, and condominium maintenance fees. In general terms, no more than 40% of your gross family income can be used when calculating the amount you can afford to pay for principal interest and taxes, plus your fixed monthly debts. The lender is naturally concerned about minimizing the risk that you will be unable to meet your financial obligations relating to the mortgage if the ratio is too high. (Refer to Sample Form #4 in the Appendix for the TDS Ratio.)

It is important for you to consider all your monthly obligations (utilities, tuition expenses for children, travel, entertainment, and so on), some of which may not be taken into account by the lender, so that you are certain about your financial standing. Complete your personal cost of living budget (Sample Form #1). This should give you some idea of what your monthly net (after tax) income is and what your monthly debt-servicing charges will be on the mortgage, plus other expenses. Also complete Sample Form #2: Personal Net Worth Statement. When you fill out

Checklist 2: Purchase Expenses Checklist, you will have a reality check of the type of expenses you need to budget for.

The Appendix also provides a list of questions (Checklist I) you can use when talking to a prospective mortgage lender.

Chapter 7

Mortgages Don't Come Cheap!

There are many direct and indirect expenses related to obtaining a mortgage. There are also additional expenses that aren't related directly to the mortgage itself. Expenses in this category include legal fees and disbursements, provincial land transfer filing fees, and property purchase tax. Other potential expenses that may be involved include a new home warranty fee, condominium maintenance fee adjustment, utility connection charges, cost of repairs that may be required prior to occupancy, and moving expenses (refer to Checklist 2: Purchase Expenses Checklist). Costs will vary considerably from one lender to another, and the type of financing that you are obtaining will be a factor. Not all expenses will be applicable in every case, but it is helpful to be aware of the possibilities.

Here is a list of some of the most common expenses that you should budget for when buying a principal residence. If you are buying investment property, depending on the type of investment property, the costs of obtaining financing could be higher. Costs also vary depending on location and province.

Appraisal Fee

The lender will have its own appraiser estimate the value of the property (its "security"), which is a factor in the size of the mortgage. The appraisal fee is paid by the borrower at the time of applying for a mortgage or is taken from the mortgage proceeds by the lender. In any event, the borrower generally pays the cost of the appraisal, although in a competitive mortgage market this is negotiable. Generally lenders will not automatically give you a copy of the appraisal, so you should arrange for a copy. Appraisal fees can range from $150 to $350.

Under certain circumstances, you may be able to avoid having an appraisal done. For example, if a vendor or purchaser has already arranged for a professional appraiser to evaluate the property, and the appraisal is not more than 60 to 90 days old, the lender may be prepared to accept the appraisal if it approves of the appraiser, and if property values have remained the same or increased since the appraisal was made. Alternatively, for example, if you are obtaining a maximum of 70% financing, many lenders will waive an appraisal requirement because the risk to the lender is less, because of the owner's equity in the property.

Mortgage Application Fee

Some lenders charge a processing fee or set-up fee for their administrative expenses in the processing of your mortgage application. Avoid paying this type of fee if at all possible. Due to the highly competitive nature of the mortgage industry, many lenders do not charge any application fee for residential mortgage purposes anyway. If you are borrowing money for real estate investment, the lender could insist you pay the fee because of the extra amount of work that might be required in assessing the loan application.

Standby Fee

Some lenders charge a fee to the borrower for setting aside and reserving the money that the borrower requires until such time as the money is advanced. The rationale behind this fee is that the mortgage company is losing revenue on this money in the interim. This fee is not commonly applied to a principal residence mortgage and you should resist paying it. It is a more common fee for money committed to real estate investment purposes or for new construction.

Credit Investigation Report Fee

This is a fee that may be charged against the borrower for the expense the lender incurs for doing credit investigation on the borrower. The fee may be either a separate fee or included in the mortgage application fee. This fee is frequently levied if you are buying investment property. If you are purchasing a home as your principal residence, however, most institutions do not charge this fee and absorb it as a cost of doing business. They intend to make money from you on the interest that you pay on your mortgage.

Survey Fee

You will generally be required to obtain a property survey prior to mortgage funds being paid out, unless you are buying a condo. The survey must be done by a qualified professional surveyor, and the purpose is to make sure that the lender knows exactly the dimensions of the property that it is using as security. The lender may also want to be satisfied that the building meets the requirements for setbacks as required by the municipal bylaws, or that any additions to the building have complied with the bylaws. The cost of the survey would be deducted from the mortgage funds that have been advanced to you, or you would pay for it directly. Your lawyer normally arranges for this survey for you. You can try to save yourself money by obtaining a survey from the previous owner, who would sign an affidavit stating that there have been no changes since obtaining the survey. Many lenders will accept this. Ask the realtor if the owner has a survey. It is primarily older houses that lenders are concerned about, due to additions, etc. If you are buying a new or relatively new house, you can ask the lender to waive the survey requirement. Survey fees range from $150 to $300 or more, depending on the property.

If you have a condominium, a survey is not required, for obvious reasons. The lender may require, though, a copy of the condominium plan showing the location of the condo you are buying.

Mortgage Broker Fee

For purchase of a home you intend to live in, it is seldom that you would be required to pay a fee for obtaining the mortgage as such. Most mortgage brokers require an advance fee, though, from you for appraisal costs and out-of-pocket costs that are incurred on your behalf. This is not the same as an application fee or administration fee, but could be included within such fees if they are charged.

If you use a mortgage broker to obtain financing *other than for your principal residence*, you may have to pay a fee, normally 1% to 5% or more of the amount of mortgage that was raised for you. This is paid at the time of closing.

Mortgage Insurance Fees (CMHC or Genworth Financial)

If you are obtaining a high-ratio mortgage or the lender requires you to obtain mortgage insurance for other reasons, then you will pay a mortgage insurance fee. The fee is approximately 0.5% to 3.0% of the amount of the mortgage that is being insured (generally the full first mortgage), and is either added onto the mortgage total or paid by you in a lump sum at the time of closing the mortgage transaction. Mortgage insurance was discussed in the previous chapter, under "High Ratio/Insured Mortgages."

Mortgage Life Insurance Premiums

Mortgage life insurance is not the same as mortgage insurance. Many of the lending institutions provide an option for you to purchase insurance that will pay off the mortgage in the event of your death, the premium for which is generally included in your monthly payments. You should compare the lender's cost with term insurance from private insurance carriers to assess if the rates are competitive. Optionally, you may prefer to protect yourself by taking out your own term insurance that would be payable to your estate in the event of your death. Your estate would then have sufficient proceeds to pay off the mortgage.

There are advantages to owning your own term insurance. It is portable (that is, you still have it after the mortgage is paid off, even if you are not medically insurable at that point). If you take out the lender's mortgage insurance policy, it only relates to paying off the balance of the mortgage. You do not own the policy separately.

In certain circumstances a lender may require, as a condition of mortgage approval, that you take out a mortgage life insurance policy; for example, if the lender felt your health were a risk factor, or if you were buying certain types of investment property. Again, you could purchase your own term insurance or other type of life insurance and verify to the lender that you had such insurance. The lender may require that it be shown on the insurance policy as being paid first from the proceeds, but this would be an unusual type of request for a principal residence. As noted, it might be more common if you were borrowing money for real estate investment purposes. As with many other expenses, you can attempt to negotiate out of the requirement.

> Note: There could be situations where you *might not be insurable* for basic term life insurance, but would be eligible for mortgage life insurance without a medical examination requirement. Your lender can advise you.

Home Fire Insurance Premium

Lenders require that any borrower on a mortgage carry sufficient fire insurance to cover the amount of the mortgage (the lender is paid first from insurance proceeds). The second and third mortgage lenders would want the same type of coverage and have documentation that they are paid off second, third, and so on. It is necessary for the borrower to purchase sufficient replacement insurance. The borrower is responsible for making insurance arrangements and paying the costs of the insurance policy showing the lender is on the policy as being paid first or second, as the case may be. This has to be provided to the lender's lawyer before any mortgage funds are advanced.

Contribution to Property Tax Account

Some lenders require that you pay 1/12th of the projected annual taxes each month. This payment is usually built into your monthly mortgage obligations, and the lender would set up a separate tax account and remit the funds directly to the municipality at the appropriate time each year. Normally taxes are payable in June or July every year, although they are calculated on the calendar year (i.e., January 1st to December 31st). Some municipalities require an advance part-payment in February of each year and the balance in July of that year.

If the lender makes the automatic monthly property tax payment a condition of mortgage approval, make sure that you enquire as to whether interest is going to be paid on your tax account to your credit, and, if so, ask what the interest rate is. The interest paid is usually lower than the interest paid on deposit accounts.

> The reason that some lenders require monthly tax payments is to minimize the risk that you will not have sufficient funds to pay the taxes every year. If this happened, the property could conceivably be put up for sale after several years of tax arrears, and this would of course compromise the lender's security.

In most cases, lenders will give you the option to be responsible for paying your own taxes directly after a year. At best, attempt to have the property tax contribution requirement waived entirely. Alternatively, you may consider monthly tax payments to be a worthwhile "forced savings" plan. If you are paying a portion of the projected property tax every month, you will have to build that expense into the costs related to your mortgage.

Property Tax Adjustment Holdback

If the lender requires that you pay a portion of the property taxes every month, and if you purchase the property on April 1st with property taxes due in July, obviously there will be a shortfall in the tax account. In other words, if property taxes are due and payable in full on July 1st and you have made payments each month of 1/12th of the projected annual tax, then by July 1st the tax account set up by the lender will be short by 9/12ths of the amount required to pay the taxes. The lender may require that you pay 9/12ths of the projected annual tax into the tax account at the time of closing the mortgage transaction. Either you would have to come up with these funds additionally or the lender would subtract that amount of money from the mortgage proceeds being made available to you. Alternatively you may be required to pay 4/12ths of the projected property tax to the lender for each of the three months of April, May, and June, prior to the tax payment deadline of July 1st.

Interest Adjustment

When you pay rent you are paying in advance. When you are pay-ing mortgage payments to the lender for principal and interest, you are paying in arrears. In other words, if you make a mortgage payment on March 1st, it is to cover the use of the funds and the interest on those funds for the month of February.

Because the lender's internal system is geared on a monthly payment basis, assuming that it is a fixed-interest rate, the lender will want to be paid in advance for the use of the funds from February 15th to March 1st. This interest adjustment is then advanced from the mortgage funds provided to you on February 15th so that the interest is prepaid up to March 1st. When your normal mortgage payment would be made on April 1st, it would cover the one-month interest charge for the month of March plus a small repayment of the principal. Not all lenders require this arrangement, but you should know in advance so that you are aware of the net proceeds that you will receive on the mortgage for your budgeting purposes.

Interest

Interest is, of course, a cost of having the funds paid to you under a mortgage.

Provincial Mortgage Filing Tax

Most provinces charge a tax or a fee for filing a mortgage in the land registry. In addition, there are filing fees for transferring title of the property. These filing fees can vary from approximately $50 to $100, or more, per filing.

Provincial Property Purchase Tax Fee

Some provinces charge a tax for transferring title in property. The tax formula varies, depending on the province. In some provinces, there is also a provincially subsidized partial rebate of that tax if you have a high-ratio mortgage.

Legal Fees and Disbursements

You are responsible for paying the lawyer for legal fees as well as out-of-pocket disbursements that the lawyer incurs relating to the preparation and filing of the mortgage documentation. Disbursements cover such things as property searches, photocopy expenses, courier costs, and other costs associated with the preparation and registration of the mortgage. The disbursement costs would normally include the provincial mortgage filing tax or fee referred to above. It is the usual practice for lawyers to deduct the legal fees and disbursements directly from the money to be advanced under the mortgage. In addition, you would obviously have to pay your lawyer to do the transfer of the property.

Sometimes, lenders require that you use a particular law firm, or you have the choice of which one of several law firms you would prefer to deal with. Other times the lender will permit you to use a lawyer of your choice. In all cases you are responsible for the legal fees and disbursements. If you are permitted to use the same lawyer to do both the mortgage and transfer, there can be savings on fees and disbursements as there is some duplication of expenses. There is also efficiency of scale.

Good and Services Tax (GST)

You will have to pay the federal Goods and Services Tax (GST) of 7% on any services that you pay for relating to your residential real estate purchase. In addition, you could pay GST on the cost of the property in some cases, for example, a new home. Check with your realtor and lawyer.

Chapter 8

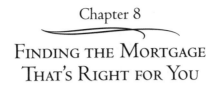

FINDING THE MORTGAGE THAT'S RIGHT FOR YOU

Key Factors to Consider When Selecting a Mortgage

Before making a final decision about your mortgage, you need to review a number of factors: amortization, term of the mortgage, open or closed mortgage, interest rate, payment schedules, prepayment privilege, and assumability. A brief explanation of each of these follows.

AMORTIZATION

Amortization is the length of time over which the regular (usually monthly or bi-weekly) payments have been calculated on the assumption that the mortgage will be fully paid over that period. The usual amortization period is 25 years, although there is a wide range of options available in 5-, 10-, 15-, or 20-year periods as well.

TERM OF THE MORTGAGE

The term of the mortgage is the length of time the mortgagee agrees to lend you the money. Terms may vary from six months to 10 years. Over a 25-year amortization period, you may possibly have several different mortgages, and, in effect, possibly 10 to 20 separate mortgage terms before you have completely paid off the loan. In reality, many people sell their principal residence or investment property after five to 10 years of ownership, depending on needs and circumstances, and buy a new property.

At the end of each term, the principal and unpaid interest of the mortgage becomes due and payable. Unless you are able to repay the entire mortgage at this time, you would normally renew the mortgage with the same lender on the same terms (subject to interest-rate changes), renegotiate the mortgage depending on the options available to you at that time, or refinance the mortgage through a different lending institution. If you renew with a different mortgage lender, there could be extra administrative charges involved. Because there is considerable competition among lenders, frequently there is no administrative fee if you are transferring a mortgage to another institution. In some cases another institution will absorb the legal fees and costs as well, as an inducement for you to bring the business away from a competitive lender. (More detail on renewing, refinancing, and renegotiating a mortgage is discussed later in Part II.)

Some people take out short-term mortgages (e.g., six months), anticipating that interest rates will go down and that at the end of that term there will be a lower interest rate. The problem is that if rates have gone up instead of down at the end of the six months, your monthly mortgage payment will increase and you may not be able to afford, or want to pay, the increased rates. The other option you have is to negotiate a long-term mortgage (e.g., five years or more years) so that you can budget for the future over a five-year period with certainty about the interest rates. The lender is not obliged to renew the mortgage at the end of the term, but in practical terms will generally do so as long as you have met your payment terms. If the lender decides to renew, an administration fee of $100 to $250 is often charged. In a competitive market, though, this could be waived.

INTEREST RATE

There are various ways to calculate the amount of interest on the loan. Two methods are the fixed rate, which means the interest rate remains fixed for the period of the term of the mortgage (e.g., one year); and the variable rate, which means that the interest rate varies every month according to the premium interest rate set by the lender every month. In this latter case, although the actual monthly payments that you would make would usually stay the same, the interest charge proportion of that monthly payment of principal and interest will vary with that month's rate.

How often interest is compounded—in other words, the interest charged on interest owing—will determine the total amount of interest that you actually pay on your mortgage. Obviously, the more frequent the compounding of interest, the more interest you will pay. The lender can charge any rate of interest, within the law, and compound that at any frequency desired. That is why it is important for you to check on the nature of the compounding of interest.

By law, mortgages have to contain a statement showing the basis on which the rate of interest is calculated. Mortgage interest has traditionally been compounded on a half-yearly basis. If a mortgage is calculated on the basis of straight interest, that means there is no compounding but just the running total of the interest outstanding at any point in time. Some mortgages, such as variable-rate mortgages, may be compounded monthly. The initial rate quoted for a mortgage is called a nominal rate, whereas the real interest rate for a mortgage compounded semi-annually, for instance, is called the effective rate. As an example, a second mortgage that quotes a nominal rate of 10% has an effective rate of interest of 10% when compounded yearly, 10.25% when compounded half-yearly, and 10.47% when compounded monthly.

Be careful when comparing interest rates when you see a rate comparison in the newspaper or on the Internet. You want to make sure that the "best rate" is not artificially low because it is based on monthly calculations rather than semi-annual interest calculations.

INTEREST AVERAGING

If you are considering assuming an existing first mortgage because the rate and term are attractive, but are concerned about the current interest rate of second mortgage financing, do an interest-averaging calculation. You might find the average interest rate to be quite acceptable. Here is an example:

1st Mortgage - $60,000 x 6% = $3,600
2nd Mortgage - $30,000 x 10% = $3,000

$90,000 x "x"% = $6,600

Average interest rate "x" % = $6,600/$90,000 = 7.3%

OPEN VS. CLOSED MORTGAGE

An open mortgage allows you to increase your payment on the principal at any time. You could pay off the mortgage in full at any time before the term is over without any penalty or extra charges. Because of this flexibility, open mortgages cost more than standard closed mortgages.

A closed mortgage locks you in for the period of the term of the mortgage. There is a penalty for any advance payment.

A straight closed mortgage will normally have a provision that if it is prepaid due to the property's being sold, a three-month interest penalty will be applied, or the penalty will be waived entirely if the new purchaser of the property takes out a new mortgage with the lending institution. Most closed mortgages have a prepayment feature. This is discussed shortly.

PAYMENT SCHEDULES

Usually payments made on the mortgage are a blend of principal and interest. These have traditionally been amortized assuming a monthly payment basis.

In terms of payment schedules, there are many options available in the marketplace, including weekly payments (52 per year), bi-weekly payments (26 per year), semi-monthly payments (24 per year), monthly payments (12 per year) and other variations. Naturally, the more frequently you make payments, the lower the amount of interest that you will be paying and the sooner you will pay off the mortgage. Some lenders give you the option of increasing the amount of your monthly payments, once a year, for example, by 10% to 20%. Other lenders have an option permitting you to make double payments. There are many different options available so thoroughly do your research.

Depending on your negotiations with the lender, you may make payments on interest only, or have a graduated payment schedule, which means that at the beginning of the term of the mortgage your payments are lower and increase over time so that at the end of the term the payments will be considerably higher. The reason for this type of arrangement is that the borrower has an expectation to earn more money over time and the payment schedules are graduated to reflect this. This could be an advantage with revenue real estate purchases or a business. There are some limitations to a graduated payment mortgage.

Many lending institutions have mortgage payment options to allow payment on a frequent basis, such as weekly, bi-weekly (every two weeks) or semi-monthly (beginning and middle of each month). Most people assume that this will automatically accelerate their mortgage debt payment significantly, resulting in the mortgage being paid off sooner and saving a tremendous amount of money in interest. This is not necessarily so. Mortgage lenders can calculate and apply the extra payments in different ways. Some ways result in very little difference in earlier mortgage payout and interest savings. Other ways make a profound difference.

To ensure that you obtain the maximum benefit, you want to make sure that your frequent payments reduce the outstanding principal by at least one extra payment a year. This in turn lowers the total interest payable on the loan, and therefore over time means more of your payments will go to reducing the principal, rather than paying the interest. The result is that you could, for example, pay off a mortgage in 17 years or sooner rather than 25 years, and save a large amount of money in interest. Remember to comparison shop and satisfy yourself that the lender's frequent payment plan reduces your mortgage at the fastest rate available, compared to the competition. Have this confirmed in writing to you.

PREPAYMENT PRIVILEGE

This is a very important feature to have in your mortgage if it is a closed mortgage. If it is an open mortgage, you can pay in part or in full the balance outstanding on the mortgage at any time without penalty. If, on the other hand, you have a closed mortgage that does not have any prepayment privileges, you are locked in for the term of the mortgage (e.g., three years) without the privilege of prepaying without penalty.

You may therefore wish to have a mortgage that, though called a closed mortgage, is in fact partly open and partly closed, permitting prepayment at certain stages and in a certain manner, but not at other times. For example, you may be permitted to make a prepayment of between 10% and 20% annually, or at any time throughout the year, on the principal or original amount outstanding, depending on the terms of your mortgage. This could be made once a year on the anniversary date of the mortgage, or at any time in that year, depending on the terms of your mortgage. Another variation would also give you the option of increasing the amount of your monthly payment by 10% to 20% once a year or at any time in the year. You can see the huge difference this would make in terms of saving on interest and reducing the amortization period. Every time you make a prepayment, or every time you increase your monthly payments, the balance owing and thus the monthly cost of interest is reduced. The net effect is that a larger portion of each payment will be applied toward the principal, since monthly (or other agreed-upon regular) payments usually remain the same. Make sure that you completely understand your prepayment options, as they could save you a lot of money. There is a considerable variance between lenders in regard to mortgage terms.

For example, you may want to have the option to pay up to 20% any time in that year, rather than waiting for the anniversary date of the mortgage; to have the prepayment amount based on the original amount of the mortgage, not the outstanding principal at the time; and to also be able to increase your monthly payments by up to 20% at any time in the year, not just to wait until the anniversary date. In other words, you want to have it all!

Another point that is important when negotiating terms is that a lender may be prepared to give you a "side letter" which confirms a modified term arrangement. For example, the lender may have pre-printed mortgage documents and a standard policy that is not as attractive an arrangement for you. The form could say 10% prepayment annually. The "side letter" could say you are permitted to pay up to 15% or 20%. If you negotiate effectively, you may be able to get the lender to modify the terms in order to remain competitive and get your business. On the other hand, its policy may not permit a modification of the standard terms, so go elsewhere. It is a highly competitive marketplace.

If you are buying a home as your principal residence, you likely will want to make use of prepayment options, especially if you know you will have extra money available from various sources. This will save you a lot of interest over time.

On the other hand, if you are buying real estate strictly for investment purposes, you may have a policy of not paying down the principal outside of the normal payments. This would preserve your cash and make it available for other purposes, for example, other real estate investments. In this scenario, you would presumably be counting on equity appreciation over time.

ASSUMABILITY

Assumability means that the buyer takes over the obligations and payments under the vendor's mortgage. Most mortgage contracts deal with the issue of assumability very clearly. The lender can agree to full assumability without qualifications, assumability with qualifications, or no assumability. For example, if a vendor reluctantly gave a vendor-back second mortgage for $50,000 for a period of two years, the vendor (the lender) may not want to have that mortgage assumed by anyone else, as the vendor would prefer to be paid out in full in the event that the property is sold, rather than carry the mortgage any longer.

The issue of assumability is an important one to consider. You would be able to have a wider range of potential purchasers interested in buying your property if purchasers who may not otherwise be able to qualify for your mortgage would be able to assume it without qualifications. Most mortgages, though, have a clause that says the mortgage is assumable *only with qualification by the lender.*

If someone assumes your mortgage, make sure you obtain a written release of any claim from the lender first. If you have already sold a home and the purchaser is to assume the mortgage, and did not obtain a release, you should be automatically released as soon as the lender extends the term of the purchaser's mortgage or varies the mortgage in any way. Check with your lawyer.

As a reminder, if you don't follow the above advice, and the purchaser assumes your mortgage and then defaults on it, you could be personally liable for the mortgage arrears.

PORTABILITY

Some lenders have a feature called portability. This means that if you sell one home and buy another during the term of your mortgage, you can transfer the mortgage from one property to the other. Check carefully, though. Some lenders require that you purchase the new house within a short period of time after you sell your original house, in order to qualify for this transfer or mortgage rate continuance option (e.g., two to four months). Other lenders require that you transfer the mortgage to your new home concurrently as you sell your old home. In practical terms, you could save money if interest rates have gone up before buying the new home. Otherwise, you would be taking out a new mortgage for your new home at current, higher mortgage rates, thereby resulting in lower mortgage amount availability.

Remember, the higher the interest rate, the lower the mortgage amount that you qualify for. Conversely, if mortgage rates have gone down since you bought the first home, you would probably not be interested in transferring your existing mortgage, unless you had a fixed-rate mortgage with a mortgage differential penalty that was larger than the savings of taking out a new mortgage.

GENERAL CONTENTS OF A MORTGAGE

Most mortgage documents are in fine print and are fairly detailed. There are no "standard" clauses in a mortgage. The only way you can fully grasp your mortgage is to have a competent and experienced real estate lawyer review it and interpret the key areas for you. In addition to differences in mortgage contracts, the laws are in a constant state of change. Many people sign mortgages without having any idea what is in them. The purpose of this section is to outline some terms that you should be familiar with so that you will be better prepared when discussing the matter with a lawyer.

In any mortgage, there are these basic provisions: the date of the mortgage; the names of the parties who are signing; a legal description of the property; the amount of the loan; the payment terms, including interest and frequency; the respective obligations of the lender and the borrower; and the signatures of all the parties. Sixteen common clauses that you may find in the mortgage are discussed below.

Personal Liability

Under a mortgage, the borrower is personally liable for the debt to the lender, assuming the mortgage is in an individual's name rather than a corporation's name. In the event of default, the lender can sue the borrower for the full amount of the mortgage; the lender is not obliged to commence foreclosure or power-of-sale proceedings and take over the property or sell the property. In practical terms, however, the lender normally commences a form of foreclosure or power of sale action to protect its interest as well as suing the borrower personally. If the property is sold, then the borrower would be responsible for the shortfall plus all the associated legal and other costs that the lender has incurred. If you have a *co-covenantor* on the mortgage (in other words, someone else who covenants or promises that he or she will meet all the obligations of the mortgage), the lender can sue both the borrower and the co-covenanter for the debt under the mortgage. (Sometimes the term *guarantor* is used instead of co-covenantor. In practical terms they are interchangeable.)

The lender may refuse to give funds covered by a mortgage without extra security protection by means of an additional guarantor or co-covenantor. If you are married and are purchasing the property under your personal name, the lender will almost always insist on your spouse's signing as a guarantor or co-covenantor, regardless of your creditworthiness. This is to protect the lender under the matrimonial or family relations legislation of the province; in the event that a separation or divorce occurs, the lender does not want its property security to be compromised.

If you have an incorporated company to purchase real estate and take out a mortgage in that name, in most cases the lender will ask you for a personal guarantee of the corporate mortgage. This makes you personally liable, of course.

INSURANCE
This clause requires that the mortgagor insure the building against fire. The insurance policy must show that the mortgagee

is entitled to be paid first (if a first mortgage) from the mortgage proceeds in the event of a claim on the policy.

There is also a provision in the mortgage that sets out the minimal amount of the insurance (replacement). It states that if you fail to pay the premium, the mortgagee can do so, or if you fail to get sufficient insurance, the mortgagee can do so, and all the additional premium costs can be added on to the principal amount of debt of your mortgage.

REQUIREMENT TO PAY TAXES

This clause states that you are obliged to pay all property taxes when they become due, and that if you do not do so, the lender is entitled to pay the taxes and add the amount paid in taxes to the principal amount of the mortgage.

Some lenders will set up a separate tax account at the time you take out the mortgage. This means that you pay an extra amount every month on your mortgage payment to the bank for a tax portion that goes into that account, and once a year the lender pays the property taxes directly. The interest paid on this money is very low, so if you can, pay the taxes yourself. Your lender will likely require proof that taxes are current.

MAINTAIN PROPERTY

This clause in the mortgage states that you are required to keep the property in good repair. The reason for this provision is that the lender obviously does not want the property to deteriorate through neglect and therefore reduce its property value, compromising the value of the security.

Occupancy

This clause is to protect the lender from owner or tenant absence for an extended period of time (for example, three months). The potential risk to the lender if no one is present in the home is that the house is subject to vandalism, arson, or deterioration. In addition, insurance coverage could be void in this situation as well, leaving the lender at risk.

Requirement to Keep Any Subsequent Mortgages in Good Standing

This provision states that you must maintain all your financial obligations on the second and third mortgages so that they do not go into default. If they do go into default, foreclosure proceedings could occur. If the property was sold, the first mortgage would be paid off first, followed by the second and the third, etc.

No Urea Formaldehyde Foam Insulation (UFFI)

Many mortgages state that no UFFI is permitted in the premises at the time the mortgage is granted or subsequently.

Prohibition Against Renting Out Premises

Some mortgage documents state very clearly that the premises cannot be rented out but can only be used as your principal residence. This can occur with some residential mortgages that are granted for the benefit of the owner/occupier and not for investment or rental purposes. In general terms, though, there are seldom restrictions against renting out a portion of your home (e.g., a "mortgage helper" in a basement suite).

ASSIGNMENT OF RENTS

If you are purchasing a revenue property, the lender may request that you sign a document entitled "Assignment of Rents." In the event that you fail to make your monthly payments to the lender, the lender can formally notify the tenants that you have assigned the rent payments to the lender directly.

COMPLIANCE WITH ALL LAWS

This provision would advise that all federal, provincial, and municipal laws concerning the use and occupancy of the property must be fully complied with. This is an important provision if you are intending to rent out the property. What happens if municipal zoning bylaws prohibit the rental of residential premises? In practical terms, most mortgage companies don't care if you rent out part of your home, even though such rental may not comply with existing municipal bylaws.

QUIET POSSESSION

This provision states that unless the mortgagor defaults, the mortgagee will not interfere in any way with the peaceful enjoyment of the property by the mortgagor. In practical terms, this means that the mortgagee cannot enter the premises.

PREPAYMENT PRIVILEGES

It is important that you make sure the prepayment privileges are set out clearly in the agreement. The various types of prepayment options were discussed earlier in this chapter.

ASSUMPTION OF MORTGAGE PRIVILEGES

Assumption of mortgage privileges should be set out clearly in the mortgage document. This subject also was discussed earlier, in Chapter 6, under "Assumed Mortgage."

Special Clauses Relating to a Condominium Purchase

These were also covered in Chapter 6, under "Condominium Mortgages."

Acceleration Clause

This clause states that if the mortgagor defaults on any of the terms of the agreement, then at the option of the mortgagee the full amount outstanding on the principal of the mortgage, plus interest, is immediately due and payable. In some provinces, legislation restricts the mortgagee from exercising the right of acceleration, even though it may be in the mortgage document.

Default

This section of the mortgage deals with the type of matters that could place the mortgagor in default of the mortgage agreement, and sets out the rights of the mortgagee in the event of default. This will be discussed in greater detail in a later chapter.

Refer to Checklist 2 in the Appendix prior to negotiating with a lender. Again, be certain that you have your lawyer advise you on the contents of the mortgage before signing it.

APPLYING FOR A MORTGAGE

In applying for a mortgage there are various steps you should follow to make sure you obtain the funds you need on the terms and conditions you want. If you go through a mortgage broker or online, some of these steps may not be required.

1. Preparation for the Application Interview

Here is a summary of the steps that you should follow prior to any interview:

a) Complete your comparison shopping of lending institutions. Check competing mortgage interest rates by contacting a mortgage broker and check their website as well as the Internet for competing sites. Refer to the business section of your local newspaper for weekly comparative mortgage rates.

b) Understand the jargon. This book should help you to know what you want from a mortgage, and therefore to negotiate the package that is best suited to your purposes. You can also refer to the Glossary in this book for common real estate and mortgage terminology.

c) Determine the questions that you want to ask the lender or mortgage broker using Checklist I as a guide, and think up additional questions that you may want to ask.

d) Determine your financial needs. Complete the cost of living budget (Sample Form #1) as well as Checklist I: Preparing for a Mortgage.

e) Calculate the maximum amount of mortgage available that you might be able to expect from a lender or through a mortgage broker or online (refer to the previous chapter). Remember, these are guidelines only.

f) Obtain a letter of confirmation of employment from your employer, if you are employed. This letter should confirm your salary, your position, and the length of time you have been with that employer. If you are self-employed, you will be required to bring copies of recent financial statements and/or income tax returns (usually the last three years).

g) Prepare a statement of your assets and liabilities and net worth (refer to the appendix for a sample form).

h) Complete the details on the amount of the down payment that you will be providing and where the funds are coming from. This last step could include savings accounts, term deposits, Canada Savings Bonds, RRSPs, a family loan, an inheritance, a divorce settlement, proceeds from the sale of a house, or other sources.

i) Obtain a copy of the agreement of purchase and sale.

2. THE APPLICATION PROCESS

a) You have to personally go to the lending institution, usually with your spouse and any co-applicant or guarantor.

b) A formal mortgage application has to be completed. The application is typically divided into three main sections: description of the property, financial details relating to the purchase of the property, and personal financial information.

c) Processing of the application by the lender normally takes between one and five business days. During that time the lender will:

- Check your credit references and your credit rating.
- Verify the financial information you have given.
- Have the property appraised (at your cost).
- Assess your application within the lender's approval guidelines.
- Issue a formal commitment of approval in writing.

d) Different lenders have different guidelines when assessing mortgage applications, but generally there are three main criteria: character, capacity, and collateral.

- *Character.* The lender will assess your credit history, and other factors as well, with a view to predicting how you will meet your obligations in the future. For example, do you pay your bills on time? What is your credit rating in terms of paying off previous loans that you have had? Do you have a dependable employment history, or have you had a different job every three or four months?

- *Capacity.* The lender is concerned about your ability to meet your financial obligation and will be concerned about such questions as: Does your GDS Ratio come within the guidelines? What are your other debts and obligations? Is your income sufficient to handle the mortgage payments? Is your income stable and does it appear as though it will continue to be so?

- *Collateral.* Lenders are very much concerned with knowing that the security that has been provided for a loan is sufficient to cover the loan in the event that it is not repaid. That is why they prefer to select the appraiser for assessing the value of a property; generally they want to have a conservative appraisal of the property as an extra caution. The lender wants to be satisfied that the property being offered as security could be readily sold if necessary. When making an appraisal and therefore determining the value of the security that is being pledged as collateral, the following factors are considered: location, price, zoning, condition of the housing unit, quality of neighbourhood, size, appearance, municipal services available, and comparative sales in the same area.

3. Pre-Approved Mortgage

The purpose of a pre-approved mortgage is to confirm in writing, in advance, the maximum amount of money on which you can rely for mortgage purposes. This exercise will help you be realistic when you are out searching for a property and negotiating a purchase.

Let's say you are offered a specific amount of mortgage for a period of time, for example, $100,000 with an interest rate that would be guaranteed for 90 days. If the rate drops before the lender advances funds, you are given the lower rate. Depending on the stability of fluctuations of interest rates, a pre-approved mortgage could range from 30 days to 120 days. Always try to negotiate the longest term. There is always a condition, of course, that the lender must approve the actual property being purchased before you can finalize the contractual offer to purchase documents, and remove all conditions. This provides the lender with an opportunity to make sure that the security is suitable.

4. Loan Approval

When the lender is in the process of approving the loan, the amount requested is an important consideration. As discussed earlier, if the amount is over 75% of the appraised value or the purchase price, whichever is lower, the mortgage normally has to be insured as high-ratio by CMHC or Genworth.

Once the lender has granted approval for the mortgage, the lender usually will have its lawyer check the title of the property to make sure that it is clear, and to perform any necessary duties, including the filing of the mortgage. Alternatively, the lender may allow the borrower's lawyer to perform the mortgage work. In either case the borrower customarily pays all the legal fees and disbursements. If you are required, or prefer, to use the lender's lawyer for preparing the mortgage documents, obtain independent legal advice about the provisions of the mortgage to make sure that the document sets out the bargain as you intend and understand it.

5. INVESTMENT OR REVENUE PROPERTY

If you are contemplating buying property other than for your principal residence, a lender is going to be more thorough in the approval process. If the investment is a house or condominium, the lender tends to be more flexible in the appraisal and lending criteria. This is because these types of real estate are relatively low risk in terms of resale potential. If you are buying a multi-unit dwelling or apartment building, the lender is very exacting and thorough in terms of the appraisal, revenue potential determination, and lending criteria. If you are buying raw land to keep or land to build on or subdivide, again the lending criterion is more stringent, because of obvious potential risks for the lender. For more information on investing in residential real estate, refer to the next chapter, and also to my book *Making Money in Real Estate: The Canadian Guide to Profitable Investment in Residential Real Estate*, Revised Edition, published by John Wiley & Sons Canada, Ltd.

Chapter 9

WHAT HAPPENS IF YOU CAN'T KEEP UP WITH PAYMENTS?

It is your responsibility to keep up with payments and keep your mortgage in good standing. As long as you do this, the lender will not commence any action to foreclose on the property or obtain an order for sale.

On the other hand, if you have difficulty making your payments or breach any terms of the mortgage, there are very severe remedies that the lender has available to protect its security (that is, your house). Defaulting on a mortgage has potentially serious consequences. If you are consistently late with your payments, you can damage your credit rating and your ability to qualify for a mortgage renewal or a new mortgage in the future.

This chapter will give you an overview of the factors that constitute default, the borrower's (mortgagee's) options, and the lender's (mortgagor's) options.

WHAT IS MEANT BY DEFAULT?

The mortgage agreement sets out in considerable detail the responsibilities of the borrower. Not meeting these responsibilities takes several forms:

- Failure to make your mortgage payments and your taxes.
- Failure to have sufficient insurance on the property, or none at all.
- Failure to obey municipal, provincial, or federal law as it relates to the premises that you have mortgaged.
- Failure to maintain the premises in a habitable (livable) condition.
- Failure to keep the premises in proper repair.
- Deliberately damaging the property that secures the mortgage.

The Borrower's Options on Default

If a mortgagee (borrower) is having difficulty maintaining payments under the mortgage, there are various options to consider:

a) Make arrangements with the lender for a waiver of payments for a period of time (e.g., three or six months) or arrange for partial payments to be made. This is usually done in a situation where the borrower is sick, injured, or laid off, or has a reduced monthly income to debt-service the mortgage due to a marital separation or a spouse who has been laid off.

b) Reschedule the debt and make new payment arrangements.

c) Refinance the mortgage with another lender on terms that are more flexible and appropriate in the circumstances.

d) Provide additional security to the lender in order to negotiate concessions (e.g., put the property up for sale).

f) Transfer the property from the borrower to the lender, obviously not a happy circumstance for the borrower.

g) Exercise your right of redemption. As a mortgagee, you are generally entitled to this right by law. This means that when you pay the arrears outstanding under the mortgage, the mortgagor is prevented from commencing or from continuing foreclosure or power-of-sale proceedings. There is an exception, however; if there is an acceleration clause, which many mortgages have, the lender is entitled to deem the full amount of the mortgage immediately due and payable. In this event, you would have to pay the full amount of the mortgage in order to stop foreclosure proceedings.

As mentioned earlier, some provinces have legislation restricting the application of acceleration clauses. In many provinces you have a right of redemption of from one to six months in order to pay the lender, or the lender would be entitled to take over the property, or sell it, among other remedies.

h) Ask the court for more time. If you can see that you are not able to pay off the lender within the right-of-redemption period, you are entitled to request of the court an extension of time. Whether the court grants an extension depends on the circumstances. For example, it is in your favour if you had previously lost your job and you are now employed, you are expecting proceeds from an inheritance, or you are having family members raise funds for you. All of these are factors that could show that the delay request is based on a realistic assessment of the ability to make the necessary payment. Having a substantial equity in the property would also assist you.

i) Put the property up for sale yourself.

THE LENDER'S OPTION ON DEFAULT

If you are in default and despite all your efforts are unable to come to terms with the lender, the lender has various options at its disposal. Generally speaking, the last thing a lender wants to do is take over the property—they are not, after all, in the business of buying and selling homes, but rather in the financing business! As well, there are other options that may be more appropriate, depending on the circumstances. The lender is required to go to the court and get approval for most of the main remedies available. That gives you an opportunity to present your side of the situation and reveal unique circumstances, if you so wish.

Legislation governing the mortgage is provincial and there can be variances between the provinces. For the most part, though, the following remedies would be available to the lender:

a) Pay taxes, maintenance fees, or insurance premiums on your behalf. The lender then adds these payments onto your total mortgage debt and charges interest on the amount.

b) Obtain an injunction from the court that you stop carrying on some improper or illegal activity. In addition, the order could require you to perform some specific obligation under the mortgage document to protect the mortgage security. You would have to pay the lender's costs of obtaining the injunction.

c) Obtain a court order to appoint a receiver of the rents, to pay the mortgage payments. This procedure is not often utilized except in serious situations involving revenue property. In reality, if you have borrowed money for revenue property, the lender will probably have had you sign an assignment of rents at the outset. The lender then can automatically notify all tenants to direct the rent payments to the lender in the event you default on the payment terms in the mortgage.

d) Obtain a court order to put the property into receivership. In this case an independent party, called a receiver-manager or receiver, takes possession of the property on behalf of the lender and maintains it. This procedure is usually utilized in the case of revenue property if other remedies are not more efficient and if the property is held in the name of a corporation, which has given the bank a debenture (a security document), or some other form of security document.

e) Accelerate the mortgage. The lender has a choice of either requesting the arrears under the mortgage or deeming the full amount of the balance outstanding on the mortgage as immediately due and payable. The lender cannot request this latter course unless there is an acceleration clause in the mortgage. Some provincial legislation restricts the use of acceleration clauses, as noted earlier.

f) Sell the property. This would mean that the lender would be able to put your property up for sale and sell it if you are in default in your payments over a set period of time. The period of time depends on the province. In many cases the lender will go through the court to get a court order for a sale so that the court can monitor the sale price and therefore minimize the risk that the borrower could claim that the house was undersold. In other cases the lender does not have to go to court to list it for sale.

g) Sue the borrower personally for the debt outstanding. The borrower is liable under the terms of the mortgage whether or not the property is sold. If it is sold, the borrower is responsible for any shortfall in what is owed to the lender. If the property is being held in a corporate name, the lender usually requests a personal guarantee of the people behind the corporation. The lender is not required to commence other actions such as foreclosure or sale of the property.

h) Foreclose against the property. In a foreclosure situation, the lender requests that the court extinguish your property rights and transfer all legal interest that you have, including the right of possession and legal title, to the lender. In this situation the lender is entitled to all equity in the property.

The courts are generally involved in this procedure and your rights are protected in that regard. For example, the court would consider it unfair if you had considerable equity in the property. It would probably advise the lender that instead of foreclosure there should be an order for sale so that the equity in the mortgage property would be able to go to the mortgagor after all the costs associated with the sale, including sales commission, the lender's legal expenses and disbursements, plus principal and interest outstanding, were paid off.

In practical terms, therefore, lenders foreclose probably less than 1% of the time. The most common method of recovery is sale of the property.

As you can see, the circumstances of your default will make a difference in terms of what steps you wish to take. Contacting the lender and attempting to negotiate a resolution is clearly the first step that you should take to resolve the problem of late payments. If that does not turn out to be a satisfactory procedure, see a lawyer who specializes in foreclosure matters so that you are fully aware of your rights and options. Your lawyer can also attempt to negotiate a mutually agreeable resolution for you.

Chapter 10

GOVERNMENT PROGRAMS THAT CAN HELP THE HOMEBUYER

Federal and provincial governments have programs that are designed to assist home ownership and/or some of the financial burdens associated with owning a home. Many of these programs have broader social and economic purposes such as to stimulate the economy, restore consumer confidence, positively affect the housing industry, better utilize existing housing, and assist those suffering from limited financial resources or assist those who are disabled. Each province has different priorities and so the types of programs and amounts of funding will differ from province to province.

Programs From The Federal Government

Here are the main federal government programs.

HIGH-RATIO CMHC-INSURED MORTGAGE

The federal government, through its Crown corporation CMHC, insures loans provided by other lenders of up to 90% and sometimes 95% of the purchase price or appraised value of the home, whichever is lower. Federal legislation requires a bank that is lending more than 75% of the purchase price to have the mort-gage insured. The higher the ratio of debt (mortgage amount) to equity (down payment), the greater the risk to the lender that if the borrower defaults on the mortgage there may not be suf-ficient equity to pay off the lender, hence the requirement for insurance protection. (Refer to Chapter 6, "Mortgage Basics," for a more detailed discussion of high-ratio mortgages.) This insurance program is therefore a form of government assistance to encourage lenders to take on extra risk in terms of providing a high-ratio loan than they otherwise might not choose to do. In other words, it is easier for you to get financing.

Government legislation has placed a ceiling of high-ratio first-mortgage financing at 90% with a 10% down payment. However, for first-time homebuyers, that would permit a loan to go up to 95% of the home value with a 5% down payment. The purpose of the program is to stimulate the economy and make it easier for people to become homeowners. With only 5% down-payment equity in the home, it is a potential risk to the lender that if the real estate market and prices dropped by 5% or more, the owner could be tempted to walk away. The advantages of the program, though, are deemed to outweigh the disadvantages.

If you are not a first-time homebuyer, you are still eligible for high-ratio insurance coverage up to 90% of the value of the purchase price. This is assuming you meet other required lending criteria.

The new homeowner program means that you can buy sooner than otherwise, as you don't have to put as much aside for a down payment. Also, the sooner you buy, the sooner you can protect yourself against future cost increases and the soon-er your investment can grow. This is assuming you buy at the right time in the market. A lower down payment can also free up your funds for other purchases such as appliances, furniture, and drapes.

Here are a few features of the programs. As these might change from time to time, check with your lender.

- Maximum mortgage loan is 95% of the lending value of the home for first-time homebuyers.
- Minimum mortgage term is five years.
- Eligible buyers would be anyone who buys or builds a home in Canada intending to occupy it as his or her principal residence, and who has not owned a principal residence at any time during the last five years. Where there is more than one buyer—for example, a marriage joint purchase—only one person has to be a first-time buyer.

Using RRSP Funds for a Down Payment

The government introduced this program to stimulate the housing industry and make it easier for people to raise a down payment to buy a home. Check with CMHC or Canada Revenue Agency for more details. The essence of the program is to permit people to tap into their RRSP funds up to a $20,000 maximum, without the withdrawal being deemed to be taxable income in that taxation year. The funds are then to be used as a down payment on a home purchase to be used as a principal residence. The key terms of the program are:

- Purchase can be for a resale home, new home, or property for the purpose of building a home.
- If the buyer is purchasing a home under construction, occupancy must take place within one year of date of purchase.

- There is a payback period for the RRSP money of a maximum of 15 years. The first payment is to occur in the first year of home acquisition, with minimum equal monthly payments over the 15-year payback period. You can pay back the RRSP money in full at any time, or make greater payments than the minimum required.

- If you don't make your required payments when they are due, the RRSP money you took out will be deemed to be taxable income in your hands in that taxation year by Canada Revenue Agency. This can be a substantial tax hit.

- You can't deduct the amount of your new RRSP contribution payments in the year that you make them, if you take out RRSP funds under this new homebuyer's program the same year, unless it is the excess of any new contribution over the amount withdrawn under the homebuyer's plan. The interest on the money you make in the new contribution that year is, of course, still tax free.

Another factor to take into account is that real estate values historically appreciate over time. Even if you must use funds from your RRSP, should you buy correctly and at the right time, your property value will rise (therefore, your equity will grow). For example, you could be making 4% on a fixed-term deposit or GIC in your RRSP that compounds tax free. At the same time, you could be saving on the amount of mortgage interest because you are able to put more money down by using RRSP funds.

If there are two first-time homebuyers (e.g., living common law or married), both parties may use their RRSP to increase the down payment.

One of the key issues to consider, of course, is that the money currently in your RRSP is generating interest which is compounding regularly (e.g., interest on the interest). All the interest accumulating in your RRSP is tax free while the funds are still in the RRSP account.

> For further information, contact your lender or the closest branch of Canada Revenue Agency, or CMHC. Also, consider exploring other alternatives than utilizing the RRSP plan. Speak to a tax accountant who can explain the financial implications in your given situation. Keep in mind that you have to balance the projected amount of lost money on the funds that you are taking out of your RRSP against the projected saving of interest in borrowing the $20,000 funds from a lender.

Partial Rebate on GST Paid

If you purchase a "used" or resale home, you do not have to pay GST on the purchase price. If you purchase a new home or a substantially renovated home, you do have to pay GST on the purchase price.

The government has a partial rebate program for those buying a home to live in, but who had to pay GST because the home was deemed to be new. There are conditions attached, however, in order to be eligible for the rebate. The home cannot cost more than a certain fixed amount. The effect of the rebate brings the GST down to about 4.5%.

Energy-Efficient Housing CMHC Mortgage Loan Insurance Premium Refund

If you buy an energy-efficient home, or make energy-saving renovations, you may be able obtain a 10% CMHC mortgage loan insurance premium refund.

Residential Rehabilitation Assistance Program (RRAP)

The program is either funded entirely by the federal government through CMHC or jointly with the provincial government. This will be clarified later. There are basically two categories of eligible recipients under this program.

For Homeowners

The purpose of this program is to assist low-income homeowners who are unable to afford adequate and suitable housing by providing financial assistance for the repair of their homes.

If your house needs repair, you may be eligible for homeowner RRAP financial assistance to help cover the cost of materials, labour, legal fees, finance costs, building plans, and permits. The assistance is provided in the form of a loan and, depending on your household income, you may only have to repay a portion.

The loan amount you may receive depends on the actual cost of repairs and where you live.

You are eligible for a homeowner RRAP if your household income is below the established "income ceilings," which vary by household size and by areas within the province. You also need to own the home and live in it. Your home also needs to lack basic facilities or require major repairs in one or more of the following areas: structural, electrical, plumbing, heating, or fire safety. If your home is too crowded and is in a rural area, you could also be eligible. Work carried out before your homeowner's RRAP loan is approved in writing is not eligible.

Contact your nearest CMHC office for more detail or check out its website: www.cmhc.ca. Program criteria and funding policies can vary at any time.

For Disabled Persons

Programs are available to assist in the modification of housing to improve the accessibility of these dwellings for disabled persons. The definition of disabled persons, in terms of entitlement to this program, is very broad. The RRAP program and others like it are available in all provinces and territories. A property is eligible if work will be undertaken to improve accessibility for a disabled occupant. The property must meet minimum standards for health and safety.

If you are a homeowner or landlord undertaking work to modify a dwelling that is already occupied by a disabled person, or that will be occupied by such a person, you may be eligible for financial assistance. This assistance can help to cover the cost of materials, labour, legal fees, financing costs, building plans, and permits. The assistance is provided in the form of a "forgivable" loan. The amount that you may not have to repay (the forgivable amount) depends on your household income.

Most modifications that make it easier for disabled persons to live independently in their homes are eligible under this program. Work carried out under this program before your loan is approved in writing is not eligible.

You may also qualify for a homeowner RRAP loan, in addition to the program for disabled persons.

Home Adaptations for Seniors' Independence (HASI)

This program helps homeowners and landlords pay for minor home adaptations to extend the time low-income seniors can live in their own homes independently.

For more information about RRAP and other assistance programs, contact your nearest Canada Mortgage and Housing

Corporation (CMHC) office, or check out their website: www.
cmhc.ca.

PROGRAMS FROM PROVINCIAL GOVERNMENTS

There are many different types of provincial government programs. Some are jointly funded with the federal government, as
noted in the previous section. Here is a sampling of programs
funded by various provincial governments.

HOMEOWNER'S PROPERTY TAX GRANT

Many provinces subsidize the property tax assessed by the local
or municipal government. There are generally three categories:
the basic homeowner's grant; a senior's grant (usually a person
65 years of age or older); and a disabled person's grant. To be
eligible, you have to reside in the home. Investment real estate is
not eligible.

SUBSIDY OF PROPERTY PURCHASE TAX

Some provinces levy a property purchase tax. If you are buying
a home as your principal residence and you have a high-ratio,
insured first mortgage, you would be eligible for a partial rebate on the property tax. There are frequently restrictions on the
maximum price of the home that governs eligibility, as well as
other conditions.

RENOVATION SUBSIDY

In addition to various federal government subsidy programs for
renovations, there are also some provincial programs. Check with
your provincial government housing department.

Property Tax Deferral

Many provincial and municipal governments have programs to permit seniors to defer local property tax payments until the house is sold. Interest accumulates on the outstanding tax balance, but the program's intent is to allow seniors to stay in their homes.

Chapter 11

Ways to Help with Mortgage Payments

There are several ways that you can offset the costs associated with owning a home. The three most common ways are renting out part of your home, taking in boarders, and operating a business out of your home. In these cases, you are eligible to deduct a portion of your home-related expenses against the income generated by the rental or business activity.

RENTING OUT PART OF YOUR HOME TO A TENANT

In this situation, you may choose to rent out a basement suite. You would be entitled to offset the rental income you receive against a portion of your house-related expenses. For example, if you received rent of $500 per month ($6,000 a year) from the rented area, and the total house-related expenses were $30,000 a year, and the rented area represented 20% of the total square footage of the house, then $6,000 of the total expenses ($30,000 x 20%) would be dedicated to the rental area. The income of $6,000 could be offset against expenses, which could meet or exceed that amount, meaning you wouldn't pay tax on that income. The usual kinds of expenses you'd claim are mortgage interest, property taxes, maintenance, utilities, and insurance. In all instances you should obtain tax advice from a professional accountant to make sure you are doing the calculations correctly.

If you are renting out part of your home, check with your provincial government to obtain information about your obligations and rights as a landlord. You would be governed and regulated by that legislation. For example, some provinces have rent control measures, while others do not. You must have a tenant agreement in writing that would deal with such issues as rent and your policy on smoking, pets, noise, and the number of people living in the suite.

Your municipality has the authority to regulate zoning and to determine whether a residence is single-family zoned. Technically speaking, you could contravene a municipal zoning bylaw by renting out a part of your home to a non-relative. In effect you would be operating as if your home were zoned as multi-family.

Check with your local municipality to determine whether zoning bylaws are enforced. If a municipal inspector does investigate, you normally have a right to appeal. One of the grounds of appeal is economic hardship for you, the owner, and serious inconvenience for the tenant. Some municipalities have a moratorium (temporary freeze) on enforcing such bylaws because of a shortage of rental accommodation, and/or general recessionary hardship of property owners that need a "mortgage helper" to meet payments. This could be because more of the owners have been laid off or otherwise are having economic hardship.

The term "illegal suite" simply means that a tenancy arrangement technically contravenes a municipal bylaw. The contravention has nothing to do with provincial legislation (dealing with landlord-tenant matters) or federal legislation (dealing with income tax). Each level of government is independent of the other.

Some provincial governments have programs to encourage home renovation in order to create rental suites. In addition, the Canada Mortgage and Housing Corporation has some programs for renovation to accommodate handicapped, elderly people, or relatives.

If you need to rent out part of your home to help meet your mortgage payments, check the policy of your lender. Some lenders (generally credit unions) will permit the anticipated rental income to be calculated as income for the purpose of mortgage qualification, especially if the suite is already rented out in the house that you are thinking of buying. Other lenders are not so flexible, on the premise that you could have an extended tenant vacancy, or that the municipality could enforce the single-family bylaw, due to a complaint, and require you to cease renting out the suite. In either situation, the lender's concern would be that you would have mortgage debt-servicing problems.

RENTING OUT PART OF YOUR HOME TO BOARDERS

In addition to a rental suite or instead of it, you may wish to take in borders if you have a spare room or two. Common facilities would be shared, such as the kitchen and bathrooms, and could include you providing some meals. You would have the same types of deductions as mentioned for renting a suite.

OPERATING A BUSINESS OUT OF YOUR HOME

Many people, at some point, intend to start a part-time or full-time business out of their homes. There is a growing trend in this area for various reasons, including eliminating the daily commute to work, lifestyle choice (e.g., to raise a family), retirement opportunity, supplementing salaried income, testing a business idea, or saving on business overhead and thereby reducing financial risk by writing off house-related expenses. There are many different types of home-based businesses.

You should solicit tax and legal advice before you start a business. Also, you may want to obtain a GST number if your annual income exceeds $30,000 or if you are paying GST on business items or services you are purchasing.

Canada Revenue Agency allows you to operate a business in your home without affecting the principal residence status, as long as you don't claim depreciation (called capital cost allowance, or CCA) on your home as part of your business operation. You can claim CCA on other non-home business capital expenditures, according to the CCA class, for example, a car or computer equipment.

There are many categories of expenses that can be deducted from income, depending on the nature of your business. An expense is deductible if a) its purpose is to earn income; b) it is not a capital nature (i.e., depreciated over time by applying CCA); and c) it is reasonable in the circumstances. Your accountant will advise you as to which expenses are deductible and which are not. Also, if some of the expenses are related to personal use, you are required to deduct that portion from the business expense.

Reasonable salaries paid to a spouse and/or children for services rendered to the business are also deductible. The "Statement of Income and Expenses" form from Canada Revenue Agency outlines some of the expenses that you may wish to consider. This form is contained in the *Business and Professional Income Tax*

Guide available from Revenue Canada. Your accountant may suggest other expenses that you could be eligible for.

You may claim expenses for the business use of a workspace in your home only if one of the following is true:

- The workspace is your principal place of business for the part-time or full-time self-employed aspect of your career (you could have a salaried job elsewhere; it is not required that you meet people at your home); or
- You only use the workspace to earn income from your business, and it is used on a regular basis for meeting clients, customers, or patients. In this case you could also deduct expenses from an office outside the home.

Note: The expenses you may deduct for the business use of your home cannot exceed the income from the business for which you use the workspace. This means that you must not use these expenses to create or increase a business loss. You may carry forward any expenses that are not deductible in the year and deduct them, subject to the same limitations, in the following year.

To deduct expenses, you must calculate the amount of space in your home that is used as an office. For example, by dividing the number of rooms in the house by the number of rooms used for business you can determine the percentage of square feet used for business. So if you are using 20% of your home for business purposes, including the basement for storage of inventory, then you would deduct 20% of all your related expenses from your business income.

There are direct and indirect expenses relating to your home business that are deductible in part or in full. As a reminder, be aware that tax laws can and do change from time to time, which could affect any of the following deductions. Here is a description of the most common expenses.

DIRECT EXPENSES

These are expenses that would only benefit the business part of the home. Some of these costs are depreciated (applying CCA) and others are deducted.

- *Room Furnishings.* Office furniture and equipment would have to be depreciated (use the CCA schedule obtained from Canada Revenue Agency). Other items such as office supplies and materials can be deducted.
- *Remodelling or Decorating Costs.* This would include repairs or renovations done to a room to turn it into an office (e.g., painting, carpentry, floor covering, plumbing, electrical, etc.). If you added an extension to your house, that would be covered as well. This should be listed as an improvement and should be depreciated.

INDIRECT EXPENSES

These are expenses that benefit both the personal and the business parts of the home business, but only the business part is deductible as a business expense. Expenses should be apportioned on a reasonable basis between business and non-business use (e.g., a percentage of the floor space used).

- *Rent.* If you rent a house or apartment and use part of it for business purposes, you may deduct the portion of your rent attributable to business use. For example, you may decide to claim 20% of your apartment or 10% of your home costs as "rent." A common range for an apartment would be from 10% to 25%, and for a house between 5% and 20%. It could be more of course, depending on use.

- *Mortgage Interest.* You can deduct the percentage of interest expense related to use of your home for business. For example, if your monthly mortgage payments are $2,000, generally almost all of that payment is interest and a small percentage goes toward the principal in the early years. This would be the case, especially in the first three years of the mortgage (assuming it is a 20-year amortization period). Therefore, for practical purposes, let's assume the interest portion is $2,000. If you were claiming 15% of your house as business-use related, you would claim $300 per month for each of 12 months, which would equal $3,600 a year as a business expense.

- *Insurance Premiums.* You can deduct that portion of insurance expense that relates to your business (e.g., fire, theft, liability coverage). If you are claiming 15% usage of your house or apartment, you would claim that portion of the premium as a business expense. Don't forget to add home office insurance to your homeowner policy.

- *Utilities.* You can deduct the portion of your expenses related to business (e.g., 15%) for oil, gas, electrical, and water costs.

- *Home Maintenance.* You can deduct a portion of your expenses for labour and material for house maintenance and repairs for business use (e.g., furnace or roof repair). However, you cannot claim your own labour. You can pay other family members for labour, as long as it is reasonable.

- *Services.* You can deduct a portion of municipal or private services such as snow and trash removal, yard maintenance, etc., for business use.

- *Automobile.* If you use a car for both personal and business travel, you need to calculate the portion of the expenses and depreciation related to business use. There are various methods of doing so and your accountant will advise you. In addition to depreciation, you can claim a portion of all other car-related expenses such as oil, gas, repairs, insurance, maintenance and interest expense, relating to financing costs.

If you have two cars, you may wish to deem one to be for 100% business use, assuming that is the case. Again, obtain advice from your accountant. Remember to have the insurance coverage include personal and business use, or all business use, depending on your circumstances. Otherwise, if you had an accident while on business matters, it could void the policy if you were not covered for business use.

- *Telephone.* If you have separate private and business lines, the full amount of the cost of the business line is deductible (e.g., monthly service charge). If you are using your residence phone for business use, you may deduct the portion of costs that is business-related. All long-distance charges that are business-related are of course totally deductible. Other phone-related costs that you could deduct (in full or in part) would be installation costs, telephone equipment, answering machine, voice mail or answering service. Use the same approach for cell phones and other communication devices.
- *Utilities.* This category includes cable TV, high-speed Internet, etc.
- *Office equipment.* This would include fax machines, computers, printers, etc.
- *Entertainment and meals.* Generally speaking, you may deduct costs incurred for business meals and for entertaining

business associates if you incur these expenses in the ordinary course of business. However, Canada Revenue Agency will accept a claim for only 50% of eligible entertainment and meal expenses.

- *Salaries.* You can claim as an expense the cost of salaries that you pay your spouse, children, or anyone else. The main criterion is that the amount you pay is reasonable in the circumstances for the service performed.

- *Education.* This category includes subscriptions to newspapers, magazines, seminars, conferences, conventions, trade shows, books, etc.

These expenses described are just some of the many tax deductions that may be available to you. Remember, you may be able to claim 100% of the cost of the expense or a depreciated amount over time, depending on the item. To clarify what you can deduct and how to do it, as well as other home business tax issues, speak to your accountant. It is also very important that you speak with your lawyer about the various types of legal issues that pertain when starting a business.

KEEPING RECORDS

If you are going to be renting out part of your principal residence to a tenant, or intend to have a home-based business, make sure that you keep detailed records (on hard copy or computerized) of all money collected and paid out. Purchases and operating expenses must be supported by invoices, receipts, contracts, or other supporting documents.

You do not need to submit these records when you file your return. If you do not keep receipts or other vouchers to support your expenses, all or part of the expenses claimed may be disallowed. Always consult a professional accountant for advice.

> If you are interested in more information about a home-based or small business, refer to my book *The Complete Canadian Small Business Guide*, 3rd edition, published by McGraw-Hill Ryerson.

Chapter 12

SOME FINANCIAL OPTIONS FOR SENIORS

Most seniors prefer to remain in their own homes as long as they can; it's where they feel comfortable and secure, and they usually have an emotional connection to home, neighbourhood, and community. They have support networks in place—through their neighbours, friends, church, or other social activities.

But some seniors simply cannot afford to stay in their homes; it is not uncommon for seniors to be house-rich and cash-poor. There are many reasons why a senior may require or need extra cash or income to supplement financial resources. Although they have contributed to private pension plans, government pensions, Canada Pension Plan (CPP), and their RRSPs, they could still experience shortfall where their income cannot meet their expenses. Other seniors may not have any savings and be relying solely on federal Old Age Security (OAS) income along with possibly a federal Guaranteed Income Supplement (GIS).

Many seniors who have fixed savings have had their purchasing power eroded by inflation. For example, with an inflation rate of 5%, which we don't have right now in this current economic environment, the cost of living doubles every 15 years. The home is the single largest form of "savings" for seniors, especially if they can tap into the equity that has accumulated, for lump-sum and/or ongoing income, without having to make monthly payments.

For many seniors, their home is their only major asset, which cannot readily be converted into income unless the home is sold and the senior moves out. Naturally, this can be a very stressful scenario. On the other hand, there are seniors who, by circumstance or choice, elect to downsize and sell the house, buy a condominium, in many cases in a retirement community, and have a considerable amount of cash left over for their financial and lifestyle needs.

There are options for seniors who want to stay in their own homes but need or wish to supplement their income. One option is to rent out a self-contained basement suite to provide income. This option may provide additional benefits in the form of companionship and security. On the other hand, some seniors may not like the loss of privacy.

UNLOCKING HOME EQUITY

There are various plans designed to help senior homeowners unlock the equity in their homes and convert that into income, or in other cases defer debt, so that existing income is not diluted. Equity is the net value of a home after all debts against the home have been deducted, for example an outstanding mortgage. If this equity can be converted into cash or income, without the owner having to sell the house and/or relinquishing possession, many seniors would be able to afford to stay in their homes. This improvement in cash flow, however, while providing a higher standard of living and meeting other personal or financial needs, may also reduce the amount available to the senior's estate. This may or may not be an issue of concern to seniors or their beneficiaries.

Housing and finances for senior Canadians is a complex topic, and must take into account lifestyle, assets, income, and taxation. This discussion does not attempt to deal with interrelated financial issues such as pension plans and income supplements or the tax implications of the various options, all of which will vary with individual circumstances. It is most important that the senior receive independent legal and tax advice from objective professionals, before any form of commitment is made. In addition, all terms must be clearly set out in writing beforehand and reviewed by your advisors to fully protect your interests.

Below is a discussion of some of the common forms of financial options for seniors. This should provide a helpful overview of the types of programs available for your own benefit or for the benefit of parents, relatives or friends who may want to consider these options. Keep in mind that programs vary from province to province and are constantly changing. Obtain a current update. Refer to the chapter on government assistance programs for further information on financial programs that could be available. Also, contact your local Canada Mortgage and Housing Corporation (CMHC) office for information on their wide range of programs, or consult their website: www.cmhc.ca.

DEFERRED PAYMENT PLANS

These types of plans involve the postponement of certain expenses until a fixed time in the future or until the house is sold. Generally, the expenses, along with any interest applicable, constitute a debt with the equity in the home as security. This is the simplest form of equity conversion. Under these plans, the senior maintains ownership and possession of the home, of course, as well as any equity appreciation. Here are some examples.

Deferment of Property Taxes

There are many seniors who are mortgage-free but who spend a significant amount of their net income on property taxes, even after any provincial homeowner's property tax grant is deducted. In addition to property taxes, there are other recurring expenses that further erode from disposable income, such as costs of maintenance, lighting, heating, water, or garbage removal.

Although property taxes are collected by and for the municipality, in most cases, some provincial governments have established property tax deferment plans. Under this arrangement, seniors are entitled to delay payment of property taxes plus accrued interest, until the home is sold or the seniors' estate is settled. Check with your local property tax department to see if such a program is available or being considered.

Deferment of Home Rehabilitation Expenses

This is a similar arrangement to the previous example, in that any loans approved for improvement or rehabilitation of the home may be deferred until the home is sold, the senior's estate is settled, or until a fixed date in the future. There are several variations of this type of program, depending on whether funds are obtained through a federal CMHC or provincial government program or a private sector funding program. Refer to the next section on reverse mortgages for a discussion of this type of plan, whereby funds can be borrowed for many different purposes (including rehabilitation expenses) with payment deferred.

Also refer to the section on government-assistance programs for home rehabilitation expense deferment. The advantage of this type of deferment is that it allows the senior to improve his or her standard of living without eroding income.

If you are considering a deferred payment plan program for yourself, or wish to suggest it to relatives, there are several key questions that you should ask:

- Is there a limit on the income of applicants to be eligible?
- Is there a subsidy of the deferral plan?
- Is there a limit on the amount of payment due (e.g., property taxes) which can be deferred?
- Is there a limitation on the time that an amount will be deferred?
- What is the interest rate charge on the amount deferred?
- How often is the interest rate adjusted, if at all, on the deferred payment? What is the formula used for determining the interest rate and how frequently is it compounded?
- If the amount of payment deferred and accrued interest eventually exceeds the value of the home, will the senior be obliged to sell the home?

Bear in mind that although property taxes are usually raised every year, and that interest rates over time, especially compounded, can erode equity in the home, these effects are partially offset by increases in the home's value due to inflation and market demand.

The Reverse Mortgage

Reverse mortgages, reverse annuity mortgages, or home-equity plans are similar concepts that are becoming increasingly popular with seniors in various communities across Canada. Over the years, seniors can build up considerable equity in their homes. Many Canadians decide to turn their largest asset into immediate cash and/or ongoing revenue and still remain in the home.

The basic concept behind these various plans is simple. You take out a mortgage on part of the equity of your home and in exchange receive a lump-sum amount of money and/or a monthly income for a fixed period or for your life and, if you are married, for the life of the surviving spouse. This latter example is sometimes referred to as a reverse annuity mortgage (RAM), as part of the money obtained from the mortgage is used to purchase an annuity. When you sell the home, or when you die, or if you are married, when your surviving spouse dies, the mortgage plus accrued interest must be repaid. You do not have to make any payments in the meantime. If there is any balance left in terms of residual equity in the home after the sale, it would belong to the senior or their estate.

You must be 62 years or age or older to obtain a reverse mortgage. The minimum size of a reverse mortgage is $20,000, but could go as high as $500,000. The cash you receive is tax-free. You do not have to make any repayments to your reverse mortgage as long as you (or your spouse) continue to live in your home.

There are many attractive features of the various reverse mortgage options. Here are some of the main ones:

- Reverse mortgages, RAMs, and other home-equity programs are readily available through a variety of agents and brokers. This permits you to compare and contrast in a competitive marketplace and end up with a plan which has features customized for your specific needs.
- The main home-equity type of plans that are available have obtained an opinion from Canada Revenue Agency that the lump-sum payment and monthly annuity payments are tax free as long as you live in your home. If you have selected a

monthly income annuity that continues after you have moved out of your home, the income from the sale may be subject to favourable prescribed annuity taxation rules. The current ruling on the various means-tested programs, such as the federal Guaranteed Income Supplement (GIS), is that receiving the annuity will not interfere with your eligibility for, or reduction in, the GIS. As tax laws and regulations change, make sure you obtain current independent advice from a tax accountant on this issue.

• As you retain ownership, you benefit from any appreciation in value of the home over time, that is, you get an increase in equity. For example, if your property goes up 10% per year in value, and you locked in the mortgage on your property for the reverse mortgage or RAM at 6%, then you are ahead at face value, in terms of the interest differential. In reality, however, because you are not making regular payments on your mortgage, the interest on it is being compounded and, in practical terms, ultimately eroding the increasing equity. The reduction could be offset substantially by an attractive average annual appreciation in property value.

Although many of the reverse mortgages, RAMs, and related plans operate in similar ways between various companies, there are variables between the plans on the issue of interest rates and other specific conditions. For example, here are some of the points to consider:

• What are the age requirements for the lump-sum or annuity plan? Do you need to have clear title on your home?
• Can you transfer the mortgage to another property if you move?

- What percentage of your home-equity is used to determine the reverse mortgage or RAM, and what percentage of that is available for a lump-sum payment and annuity?
- Is the interest rate on the mortgage fixed for the life of the senior or duration of the annuity, or is it adjusted; if so, how regularly and using what criteria?
- If the reverse mortgage and lump-sum amount is for a fixed-term period, what are the various terms available?
- What if the equity of the home on sale is insufficient to pay the mortgage and accrued interest? Are the seniors or their estate liable for the shortfall?
- Can the agreement of the term be extended if the home has appreciated in value?
- Can the senior move out of the house, rent it, and still maintain the home equity plan?
- What if the senior already has a mortgage on the house?
- If the annuity is for life, is there a minimum guaranteed period of payment or will payments stop immediately upon the death of the recipient and/or the surviving spouse?
- How will the income received under the proposed plan be taxed?
- Will the income received affect the eligibility of the senior under any federal or provincial housing or social programs?

The process of obtaining a reverse mortgage or RAM takes about four to six weeks, on average. This would include home appraisal, annuity calculations, and other matters. As mentioned, as these plans are fairly complex, it is essential you obtain independent legal and tax advice in advance and thoroughly compare the features and benefits, and that you only take out the right amount of equity for your needs.

SELLING THE HOME TO AN INVESTOR

In this arrangement, seniors convert all their equity into income by selling the home outright to an investor, but continue to live in the home. Sale plans generally take place between homeowners and individual investors, not financial institutions.

Compared to a reverse mortgage arrangement, a sale plan has the advantage of freeing up all the equity in the home, not just a portion of it. One of the key disadvantages, though, is that any future appreciation of value in the home over time is lost, as the home would be owned by someone else. This may or may not be an issue or cause for concern to you, depending on your circumstances. The payment of the cash equity in the home can be structured in different ways. For example, you could receive a lump-sum amount equal to the present value of the home, or in some cases a reduced value of the home. You may wish to use the funds to buy an annuity. Another example would be a regular monthly income for a fixed period or for life, with or without an annual increase factor to allow for inflation. A third option is a combination of the two just described.

There are various ways that a sales plan could be structured.

1. Sale Leaseback

One option is an arrangement whereby the senior agrees to rent the house from the investor after the purchase is complete. This is commonly referred to as a sale leaseback. The ownership in the property is transferred to the investor and the seller receives a lump-sum payment or regular monthly income. The seller pays rent on a monthly basis to the owner and is entitled to continue to rent for the life of the senior or surviving spouse, or for a fixed term.

There are a range of issues and areas of potential risk associated with a sale leaseback:

- It may be more beneficial, as well as less risky, for the owner to take a lump sum and purchase an annuity with part of it. The benefits would be that the owner has the full amount of sale proceeds that he or she controls, and can negotiate the best annuity program from the marketplace.
- The risk of agreeing to receive regular monthly payments from the investor, instead of a lump-sum, is that the investor may default on payments or go into bankruptcy. Keep in mind that the owner has the title to the property, and in theory could mortgage the property for other business purposes, default on those obligations and risk placing the house in foreclosure. There are ways to attempt to protect this from occurring by having a mortgage placed in the senior's favour against the property to the amount of the balance outstanding to the senior. Seek legal guidance.
- If you are considering the possibility of agreeing to monthly payments, you should also deal with the issue of what happens in the case of death or failing health requiring a move to hospital care before the term is up. How is the issue of compensation to the senior or estate of the senior dealt with? There would still be money owing to the senior. Another issue is whether the senior has the right to sublet the premises in the case of the senior wanting to leave the home, due to illness or for other reasons.
- If the lease is for a fixed term, rather than for life, the investor could increase the rent at the end of the term, which could be more expensive than what the senior can afford. One way around this is to have a fixed rent until the end of the term,

and then a formula for increasing the rent annually thereafter, for example at 3% per year. The investor may not want to commit to an arrangement that would allow you to pay less than market rent without offering you a reduced amount for the original purchase price to compensate for it.

- In view of the fact that the investor now owns the property and is, in effect, the landlord, it should be clearly set out in writing that the investor is responsible for repair and maintenance, property and other municipal taxes, insurance, and heating and lighting expenses.

- The senior should be satisfied, by obtaining independent legal and tax advice, that the purchase price offered and the proposed rent reflects fair market value.

- If the senior is going to obtain a monthly income from the investor, the issue of how that income is going to be taxed, if at all, has to be dealt with. Another issue is how the income might affect any provincial or federal government financial benefit program that the senior would otherwise be entitled to.

2. Life Estate

This concept means that the senior sells the home to an investor but maintains ownership and can remain in the home rent-free for life or, if a couple, the life of the surviving spouse. The investor obtains ownership on the death of the senior. The senior is responsible for all expenses relating to homeownership, of course, such as repair and maintenance, insurance, property and other taxes, and utility costs such as heating and lighting. In addition, the senior would normally be able to make decisions as any homeowner would do, such as deciding to move out and rent out the home, or do interior decorating.

Because the investor is permitting the owner to live in the house without paying rent, the price paid for the house will be less than full market value. How much money is deducted for the value of the life estate at the outset is based on a number of variables. For example, the age, health, sex, and marital status of the senior are all factors which are taken into account when projecting how long the life expectancy of the senior might be, and therefore how much discount to take off the fair market value of the home.

The cautions and potential risks related to a life estate arrangement are similar to those discussed earlier relating to the sale leaseback option.

You can see the wide range of financing options available to senior Canadians. As a reminder, make sure you obtain independent legal, tax, and financial advice before you commit yourself to any type of program.

Chapter 13

CREATIVE FINANCING SECRETS

Yes, you can get creative about financing a property. Here are a few tips.

CREATIVE FINANCING—TELL ME MORE

Sometimes the only way to make a particular deal work is with creative financing. This means that the financing is constructed legally but in ways not commonly used. The "standard fixed payment" bank mortgage, for example, falls under traditional financing. In that type of financing, a regular payment is made monthly, with the interest due applied first and the balance to the reduction of the principal.

Optionally, here are some creative financing techniques:

- *Interest Deferral.* Interest is calculated as usual but payment of the interest is delayed. This is sometimes referred to as a balloon payment mortgage.
- *Equity Participation.* In exchange for lending money with attractive terms, the lender shares in the price increase (equity) in the property.

- *Mortgage Assumption.* Rather than taking out a new mortgage, the purchaser assumes the existing mortgage of the vendor. The vendor should negotiate a full release of any future obligations under the mortgage.
- *Variable-Rate Mortgage.* The interest rate is adjusted according to an index (e.g., prime rate) at certain intervals and frequently with a limit on the amount of interest. Terms and payment may be adjusted.
- *Reverse Mortgage.* Owners of property with substantial equity can receive regular monthly payments that have to be repaid at a later time, generally at the time of house sale or upon the death of the debtor. In effect, it is similar to an annuity. Seniors and retirees tend to find this a popular program. This is discussed in more detail in the chapter on financing options for seniors.
- *Graduated Payment Mortgage.* Here, payments start at a lower monthly amount and gradually increase over time. Over the term of the mortgage (e.g., five years), the monthly payments could average out. This mortgage is sometimes preferred by people who have investment property, but want to avoid negative cash flow. The monthly payments therefore increase with the monthly cash flow over time.

DEALING WITH NEGATIVE CASH FLOW

If you are a real estate investor, you are naturally going to be concerned about negative cash flow—that is, a shortfall every month in terms of monthly financial obligations. In others words, rent does not meet mortgage and related expenses. A common cause is unit vacancies. You would normally have to subsidize the shortfall yourself. The negative cash flow could be temporary and is sometimes justified. Each situation is unique.

There are different ways of avoiding or dealing with the issue of negative cash flow. Here are some methods:

- *Rent with Option.* The tenant pays an extra premium every month over the base rent, along with an option to purchase. The overage would be deemed a down payment by the vendor on eventual sale. In the meantime, the vendor has eliminated the cash flow shortage. If the renter does not exercise the option, the overage is deemed a fee for the option and is not returned to the renter.
- *Equity Sharing.* Basically, it means the renter pays a monthly premium and shares in the equity build-up when the property is sold. Generally, the renters also have a first option to buy.
- *Graduated Payment Mortgage.* As explained above, it is an effective way of dealing with negative cash flow.
- *Purchase a Lower-Priced Home.* Obviously, one way of dealing with the problem is to reduce the amount of negative cash flow by having a lower monthly debt.
- *Rent Out a Suite.* If you have an investment property with a self-contained suite, rent it out separately.
- *Refinance the Property.* If interest rates have dropped, you may be able to refinance the property. Even if you have to pay a penalty on a closed mortgage, you could still be further ahead over time in terms of the savings. Your calculations will reveal the cost/benefit. Also consider locking in a long-term fixed-rate mortgage (e.g., five years) if interest is at an attractive rate.
- *Rent to Singles.* You can probably generate considerably more revenue by renting a house to, say, six single individuals rather than to a married couple with a family. The extra revenue

could eliminate any negative cash flow. Careful selection of the renters and monitoring should minimize the risk of renting to a number of unrelated people. Make sure you have a tenancy agreement signed dealing with issues such as no pets, no smoking, no excessively loud parties, and the number of people who can reside in the property.

- *Obtain a Longer Amortization Period.* As you know, the longer the amortization period, the lower the monthly rates. So a 30-year period will result in lower payments than a 20-year period.
- *Reduce Expenses.* Review all the expenses that are being incurred, and look for ways of reducing them.
- *Negotiate a Lower Purchase Price.* If you know in advance (which you normally should, of course) that you are going to have a shortfall, use that as leverage to attempt a price reduction.
- *Pay a Larger Down Payment.* Clearly this will reduce the monthly debt servicing and reduce or eliminate the cash flow shortfall.

For more information on real estate investment strategies, refer to my book, *Making Money in Real Estate: The Canadian Guide to Profitable Investment in Residential Property*, Revised Edition, published by John Wiley & Sons Canada, Ltd. Also refer to the website www.homebuyer.ca.

Chapter 14

Renew, Refinance, and Renegotiate

At some point, the term of your mortgage will come due and you will have to consider the options available to you, including renewing or refinancing. Alternatively, you may want to renegotiate your mortgage before the end of its term because of lower interest rates in relation to the interest rate your mortgage is bearing. If you have an open mortgage, you have more options than if you have a closed mortgage.

RENEWING A MORTGAGE

When your mortgage term expires, the full amount of the outstanding principal plus any accrued interest is deemed to be immediately due and payable. Various options will be open to you, including renewal for a further term. Here are the various facts to keep in mind, and the steps to follow.

1. No Automatic Right to Renew

Many people assume they can automatically renew their mortgage at the end of the term, subject to any interest rate change for a new term. This is not so. The lender can refuse to renew the mortgage for several reasons:

- Interest rates have gone up substantially to the extent that the borrower does not technically qualify for the amount of the mortgage in terms of debt-servicing ratios. Remember the discussion of GDS and TDS ratios in an earlier chapter.
- The value of the property has decreased, resulting in an increase in the debt-to-equity and thereby reducing the lender's security and increasing the lender's risk.
- The financial situation of the borrower has changed; for example, through marital separation, illness, injury, or loss of a job and therefore the borrower's overall income and debt-servicing capacity has dropped.
- The borrower has developed a history of missed payments, late payments, or returned (NSF) cheques.
- The lender's lending policy has changed.

In practical terms, though, as long as you have maintained your monthly obligations, the lender will renew your mortgage for another term, subject to any changes in current terms or interest rates. There are obvious advantages to the lender to do so. Over the years, a degree of trust has developed between the parties. It is time-saving for the lender not to have to review a new mortgage application or appraise the property. And, of course, the lender is making money on the interest rate spread between what the bank is charging you for the mortgage and what it is paying for deposit funds.

2. OFFERING OF RENEWAL

Prior to the end of the mortgage term, referred to as the "maturity date," the lender will generally send you a notice advising you that you will be offered a renewal and setting out the various options, such as current open- and closed-term periods (e.g., six months, one-year, three-year, five-year, etc.). In addition, the renewal fee costs are set out.

3. Options on Receiving Renewal Offer

You have various options at the end of the term. You may:

- Reduce the principal by making a partial prepayment, without a penalty. If you had the funds, you could even pay off the balance outstanding in full without a penalty.
- Reduce the amortization period on which your regular payment is calculated, for example, from the "standard" 25-year amortization to a 20-year or 15-year amortization. Your monthly payments will, of course, go up accordingly. The lender may charge a modest fee for this change.
- Change the frequency of your payments.
- Increase the amount of the mortgage. Many lenders will lend you an additional amount at renewal time, if you have increased equity and can afford the increased monthly payments. The funds could be for renovating or paying off other debts. Refer to the next section on refinancing.
- Transfer the mortgage to another lender. In practice, this means that one lender will advance funds to pay off and then discharge the other lender's mortgage, and replace it with its own. Refer to the next section on refinancing.
- Assign the mortgage to another lender. This means that one lender pays off the other and then assumes the existing mortgage. Refer to the next section on refinancing.

4. Accepting the Terms of the Renewal

If you decide to accept the renewal from your current lender, there are various steps:

- Select the term, interest rate, and payment frequency from the options set out by the lender.
- Negotiate any other features or terms you would like modified (e.g., amortization period or obtaining more funds).
- Sign the formal renewal agreement or a new mortgage document. In most cases, the lender has you sign a renewal agreement modifying the terms of the original mortgage. This is not normally registered in the land registry office. Your existing mortgage is still filed there. Also, you normally don't need a lawyer to witness your signature. Occasionally, the lender has you sign a new mortgage document if there have been substantial changes to the original mortgage document. This would normally be registered in the land registry office against your property.
- Return the renewal agreement to the lender before the maturity date deadline. You would also pay the renewal fee, which tends to be nominal (e.g., $50 to $150+, depending on the lender).

REFINANCING

For any number of reasons, you may want to find a new mortgage company or completely renegotiate the arrangement with your existing lender. Another lender may have a far more attractive package for you than your existing lender, for example, by offering prepayment or multiple payment options, or lower interest rates. Refinancing means paying off the existing mortgage and arranging for a new mortgage with the same or a different lender.

To refinance will normally incur the same costs as you incurred for the original mortgage, as the new mortgage company is going to have to prepare and register its own mortgage. This would include appraisal, survey, and legal costs. In practice, though, due to the competitive nature of the mortgage industry, lenders may offer many incentives to attract your business, such as special package rates for all legal and associated fees for transferring (e.g., $500, or eliminating any fees and costs altogether). In other words, the lender would be making all the arrangements for you, so it is stress-free and convenient.

Another common incentive for lenders is to waive any requirement for you to pre-qualify, or absorb the cost for an appraisal or survey. This would be on the assumption, of course, that property values have not gone down since you obtained your original mortgage.

If you are refinancing the mortgage at the end of the term of the mortgage, it is a relatively simple procedure. If you are using a different lender, you would pay off the existing lender plus a discharge preparation fee, usually $50 to $100+, plus your legal fee to file the discharge. If you want to refinance before the end of the term, due to a change in interest rates or other factors you want to take advantage of, consider whether you have an open or closed mortgage. If you have an open mortgage you are entitled to make additional payments to reduce or pay off the principal at any time. On the other hand, if you have a closed mortgage, it is a different matter.

PREPAYING A CLOSED MORTGAGE

As you know by now, a closed mortgage means that, in almost every case, you are not allowed to prepay any of the principal at any time during the term of the mortgage without having to pay a penalty. For example, if you have a one-year term, the lender is not obliged to accept any payments from you except for principal and interest monthly payments.

In practice though, most residential mortgage lenders include a prepayment privilege, even in a closed mortgage. (This was discussed in Chapter 8, under "Key Factors to Consider When Selecting a Mortgage.") In the case of CMHC-insured closed mortgages, there is generally a prepayment of 10% of the principal balance permitted, and only on the anniversary date of the mortgage. There is also a provision that if the mortgage term is three years or more for a CMHC-insured mortgage, the borrower can prepay the mortgage with a three-month interest penalty after three years. Under the Interest Act of Canada, any residential mortgage with a term of five years or longer can be prepaid at any time after the fifth year with a three-month interest penalty. As regulations can change, satisfy yourself that these guidelines are still current.

Most lenders have prepayment conditions that state that there is a three-month interest penalty, or an interest differential charge, whichever is greater. The interest differential is not a problem when interest rates are going up, but only when they are going down. Let's look at these penalties:

Three-month Interest Penalty. As you probably know, especially in the first three years of a mortgage, almost all the monthly mortgage payments go to paying interest and very little is applied towards principal. In fact, about 95% of payments in the early years goes towards interest. Therefore, in practical terms, a three-month interest penalty effectively means three months of mortgage payments.

Interest Differential. There are various technical definitions of this. In simple terms, it is the money that the lender would lose, if any, between the interest rate that you are currently paying and the market interest rate that the lender would be receiving at the time you prepaid the mortgage, for the duration of the mortgage term. For example, if you have a three-year closed mortgage and want to prepay it after year one, you will have two years left on the term. If you are paying 6% on the mortgage and the current market rate for a two-year closed-term mortgage (the balance left in your term) is 8%, then the lender is not losing anything from the differential, and in fact will make money by lending it out again at a higher rate. The lender will therefore opt for the three-month interest penalty.

On the other hand, if the current interest rate is 4% for a two-year closed term, the lender will be losing money if you prepay your closed mortgage in full. It would represent a 2% differential loss (from 6% to 4%). The actual monetary loss can be calculated. Let's say, in a hypothetical example, the lender's loss would be $20,000. That is what you would pay the lender for prepayment, as it would presumably be greater than the three-month interest penalty amount. If you have a prepayment privilege feature in your mortgage where you can prepay, for example, 20% of the original principal amount of the closed mortgage at any time in the year, then you would pay the interest differential penalty on the net amount, after a credit is given for the permitted prepayment portion noted above. You can appreciate the significance of these features.

If you are taking out a new closed mortgage for a three- or five-year period, you can see the importance of looking at the issue of prepayment privileges and prepayment penalty. It will make a considerable difference in the interest you can save with partial prepayments. It will also impact on the amount you would have to pay if you prepay in full and there is a high interest differential because of a large increase in interest rates.

If you are considering prepaying your closed mortgage in order to refinance, because of more attractive interest rates, check your mortgage agreement and do your calculations thoroughly. Get advice from your lender, lawyer, and a mortgage broker. You have to weigh all the advantages and disadvantages. If the cost is too great, you may want to take advantage of other options that you have in your mortgage to save on interest, for example, by paying the most you can on prepayment privileges and making more frequent payments.

If, for various reasons, you are obliged to prepay a closed mortgage, there are various options that may minimize or even eliminate the economic pain.

- Have the purchaser of your home assume your mortgage. This would avoid a prepayment penalty. Make sure you obtain a release from your lender of any mortgage responsibilities in case the purchaser defaults on the mortgage; otherwise, you could still be liable under the original mortgage, in many cases. If your mortgage rate is higher than the prevailing interest rate, you could have a problem enticing a purchaser to assume the mortgage. The exception would be where the purchaser might have difficulty getting sufficient mortgage financing otherwise and wants to buy your home. The lender, of course, has the right in most cases to approve the mortgage being assumed, subject to the purchaser passing certain qualifying requirements.

  Alternatively, you could attempt to entice the purchaser by reducing the purchase price of the home but not as much as the penalty, offering a small vendor-take-back second or third mortgage to facilitate the purchase, and/or pointing out the advantages of a wrap-around mortgage.

- If you have a portable feature to your mortgage, move it to your new home. This would avoid a penalty. If your mortgage interest rate is higher than the prevailing rates, the wrap-around mortgage could make your payments easier. If your existing mortgage rates are close to or lower than the prevailing rates, then you could be further ahead because of saving on the penalty and/or saving money on the interest rate.

- If you are close to the expiration date of the term—for example, 30 months into a three-year (36-month) mortgage— many lenders will just charge you one month's penalty, not the three months they otherwise might be entitled to. This would be part of your mortgage document, and one of the features that you should consider in your initial mortgage selection.

- Negotiate with your mortgage lender. Depending on your circumstances, some lenders might be prepared to lower your interest rate or permit the payout of a reduced penalty. Convince the lender of the overall benefits of having you remain as a customer. Perhaps you have other accounts with the lender or RRSPs, or have been a long-time customer. Also, the lender would be making money on a mortgage with you if you remain with them, but at a lower interest rate. If it was possible for you to refer the new purchaser of your home to your lender for a mortgage, that would also be a selling point.

- Ask the lender to waive the penalty. If interest rates have increased substantially, the lender could be grateful for the opportunity to lend out your money at a much higher return. It would therefore be in the lender's best interest to facilitate your refinancing.

- Check the terms of your mortgage thoroughly. It could be that you are entitled to pay your mortgage off with a three-month penalty rather than a larger penalty or interest differential, because of the fact it is, say, a CMHC-insured mortgage.

- If you are suffering from financial hardship due to job loss, marital separation, or health problems, bring those factors to the lender's attention. If the lender realizes that you are compelled to sell your home, this could result in a review of the penalty provision.
- If you fail to meet your payments, the lender may begin legal demands and subsequent litigation against you to recover the outstanding amount of principal, interest, and legal costs. If the lender demands the full amount of the mortgage from you, rather than just the arrears, this normally has the effect of cancelling any claim against you for a penalty.

The prepayment penalty is there as a disincentive for you to pay down the mortgage in full before the end of the closed term. If the lender is the party demanding the full payment of the mortgage, that is a different matter. Of course, once you are in arrears and/or subsequent legal action is commenced, that will generally show up in a credit bureau report and therefore affect your credit rating, plus your ability to readily obtain new mortgage financing. For more detail refer to Chapter 9, "What Happens If You Can't Keep Up with Payments?"

In all these cases, make sure that you obtain advice from a lawyer who can review the mortgage document and circumstances and counsel you on your options, rights, and responsibilities.

RENEGOTIATING A MORTGAGE

This simply means changing the existing terms and conditions of your mortgage agreement with the lender. Because the lender is relying on your contract, renegotiation may not be possible or may have a fee attached. The policy and charges depend on the lender. The discussions above relate to forms of renegotiating.

Chapter 15

INVESTING IN MORTGAGES

Most people understand the concept of mortgages from the viewpoint of the borrower. But mortgages can often offer attractive potential *as an investment*. There are several ways of investing in mortgages. Depending on the option, you have to take various issues into serious consideration. These include:

- your personal preferences and objectives
- your income-tax situation
- the degree of risk involved and your risk tolerance
- return on investment
- amount of control you have over the investment
- degree of liquidity required
- nature of security
- time required to administer the investment, if any
- your stress tolerance (comfort level)
- your past investment experience
- the nature of potential mortgage investment
- the advice of your lawyer and accountant (and financial planner, if you have one)

This chapter will briefly discuss the most common investment options and cautionary tales. The options include NHA mortgage-backed securities, mortgage mutual funds, self-directed RRSP mortgages, mortgage brokers, private mortgages, and real estate investment trusts (REIT). *It is essential that you obtain professional and objective advice before you commit yourself.*

NHA MORTGAGE-BACKED SECURITIES

The federal government, through the National Housing Act and administered through Canada Mortgage and Housing Corporation, offers mortgage-backed securities (MBS). These securities are a combination of direct investment in an undivided interest of a pool of residential first mortgages, insured through CMHC, and government bonds. As an investment, therefore, they are comparable to top-quality government bonds and have the advantage of higher yields (return on your investment) which result from CMHC-insured first mortgages.

MBSs are among the safest of all investments. The securities are insured through CMHC for the full amount of principal and interest in the event of mortgage default. Also, timely payment on the 15th of each month is guaranteed by the government, whether or not payments are made on the underlying mortgages. The mortgages themselves are secured by the value of the underlying real estate. As an investor, you would be buying into a pool of perhaps 100 residential mortgages. The NHA also has other types of pools available, such as multiple project or social housing mortgages.

All mortgages in the pool are based on blended equal payments.

The payments you receive are made up of interest, principal, and prepayments. In the event the original borrower of the mortgage funds prepays the mortgage, all prepaid principal, along with any penalty, is immediately returned on a prorated basis (proportionate to the investor's interest) to the investors in the next monthly payment. You can now see why there is a penalty for prepayment of a closed mortgage—investors want to be able to rely on a certain amount of interest. To compensate for the interest that the investors would lose if the closed mortgage were paid off before the end of term, there is frequently an interest differential penalty. Alternatively, there would be a three-month interest penalty.

You can also see why an open mortgage has a higher interest rate. The investor knows the mortgage can be paid back at any time without penalty, which adds a degree of uncertainty as to whether the interest payments will continue to the length of the mortgage term; the interest rate is higher as compensation for this uncertainty.

The minimum purchase price for an MBS investment unit is $5,000. MBSs are usually issued for five-year terms. This certificate, like a bond, can be readily sold before maturity on the secondary market at par, at a discount or at a premium, depending on how its yield currently compares with similar investment options. This liquidity (ability to cash in quickly) is an important feature. Like Government of Canada bonds, NHA MBS prices in this secondary market tend to fluctuate with changing interest rates, declining as interest rates rise and rising as interest rates fall. An NHA MBS may be included in any RRSP fund portfolio or as part of a self-directed RRSP. They are also eligible for RRIFs. Traditionally, NHA MBS investments provide a higher interest yield than Canadian government security of comparable maturity. Because an MBS is an interest-rate-sensitive security, the return on it is determined by prevailing market conditions.

There are significant differences between NHA MBS issues and Guaranteed Investment Certificates (GIC) issued by banks.

GICs do not have the government guarantee through CMHC that is standard on an NHA MBS issue. Also, the underlying mortgages in an NHA MBS are fully insured by CMHC. The timely payment guarantee of all principal and interest, regardless of the amount, compares with a maximum of just $100,000 of Canada Deposit Insurance Corporation (CDIC) on GIC investments. In addition, GICs are not tradable on the secondary market.

If you wish to consider this type of investment, you can obtain further information on how to buy or sell an NHA MBS from your nearest branch of CMHC, or through investment dealers, stockbrokers, banks, credit unions, or financial advisors.

> It is informative to view mortgages from an investor's perspective. It shows you where lenders source a major amount of funds, which they lend out as mortgages. This applies to CMHC or the traditional lenders such as banks and credit unions.

MORTGAGE MUTUAL FUNDS

Most banks and credit unions have mutual funds available that invest primarily in a pool of high-quality residential first mortgages. The mortgages, in theory, could be those of your neighbours, your friends, or even your own. Your return on your mutual fund investment is primarily in the form of interest payments made on those mortgages. This investment is therefore similar to the government-guaranteed form of mortgage-backed security, except that if the mortgages used are high-ratio mortgages, they would be insured by Canada's only private mortgage insurance company, Genworth.

These types of mortgage mutual funds can be attractive to those who want to place their investment where it is secure, with a record of generally dependable returns and steady growth. In addition, they have liquidity. In other words, you have the ability to cash in part or all of your holdings at any time if you need money. Naturally, investment returns will fluctuate as mortgage interest rates fluctuate.

Mortgages are carefully screened to ensure that any risks are kept to an absolute minimum and managed in such a way to take advantage of the rise and fall of interest rates. For example, if interest rates are high, the fund managers would generally select mortgages with longer terms wherever possible, thereby locking in good yields (return on investment) for several years. As a result, mortgage funds are more stable than bond funds in times of volatile interest rates. This limits the capital gains potential of a mortgage fund, but it also means greater stability in unit values if rates rise. Units can be purchased for as little as $500.

Generally speaking, there are no sales commissions of any kind to pay when you invest (referred to as a no-load fund) and no redemption fees if you cash in your units. There is the expense of an annual management fee, which could range from approximately 1% to 2%. The mutual fund is RRSP eligible; funds held within an RRSP are generally subject to an additional small fee.

As the mortgage fund market is very competitive and fees and returns can vary, do your research thoroughly. Make sure you comparison shop if you wish to consider this form of investment to add to your balanced investment portfolio. Ask for the past history of investment returns. Past performance, of course, is not a guarantee of future returns. Get professional advice that takes your individual circumstances into account.

SELF-DIRECTED RRSP MORTGAGES

You are undoubtedly aware of what a Registered Retirement Savings Plan (RRSP) is. It is a fundamental part of prudent personal retirement planning. You probably have an RRSP plan now that you pay for directly or through monthly salary deductions through your company. For those who are not familiar with an RRSP, it is a type of savings plan to which you can contribute a portion of your earnings and receive a tax deferral on that amount, and you can actually deduct the RRSP payment from your taxable income, thereby reducing the tax you pay each year.

Your non-RRSP earnings are taxable every year. When you eventually take out the RRSP funds, either before or after retirement, and either in part or full, you are taxed on them at that point in that taxation year. As your taxable income is presumably lower in your retirement years, the amount of tax you would pay on your RRSP withdrawals would be less.

Another major advantage of an RRSP is that the interest on the RRSP amount is not only compounding, but it is tax-free while in the RRSP. The term "compounding" refers to the payment of interest on the principal amount plus any interest already earned. For example, if you had $1,000 invested at 6%, you would earn $60 in the first year of the investment. At the start of year two, therefore, interest would be paid on $1,060. This is assuming your interest is calculated annually. If it is calculated semi-annually or monthly, the interest earned would be greater than $60, due to the interest being added to the principal more frequently than once a year. Therefore, more "interest on interest." This is the benefit of compounding.

There are many factors to look for in an RRSP, such as flexibility, safety of principal, return on investment, and sales fees and charges. There are basically two types of RRSPs: a managed RRSP and a self-directed RRSP. In a managed RRSP, your funds are invested by an institution such as a bank, credit union, life insurance company, management company or investment dealer.

Most plans fall into five categories:

- Guaranteed Plans: These are usually offered by banks, trust companies, and credit unions and involve "no risk" investments locked in at a set rate for a set term.
- Bond Plans: A bond plan consists of a diversified portfolio of high-quality bonds.
- Equity Plans: A diversified plan consisting of a portfolio of primarily Canadian stocks.
- Balanced Plans: A combination of an equity plan and a bond plan.
- Mortgage Plans: Assets are invested in a portfolio of mortgages.

A self-directed RRSP is one in which you make your own investment choices for your plan, usually with the help of a registered representative. A trustee handles all of the administrative details, for which you pay a fee, of course. There are various kinds of investments that you can make in a self-directed RRSP. Here are the key ones that Canada Revenue Agency has approved:

- bonds and debentures of Canadian governments and Crown corporations
- shares and debt issued by corporations listed on a Canadian exchange
- rights and warrants listed on a Canadian exchange
- units of a qualified mutual fund trust
- guaranteed investment certificates issued by a Canadian bank, trust company, credit union, or other financial service company
- treasury bills
- mortgages

Investments such as gold and silver bars, commodities futures contracts, art, antiques or gems do not qualify.

Generally speaking, mortgages qualify for self-directed RRSPs. This would include your own mortgage, as well as mortgages that you hold other than your own; for example, a first, second, or third mortgage that you have been given in exchange for lending money out privately, or possibly you purchased an existing mortgage. (Holding a private mortgage is covered later in this chapter.) When dealing with a mortgage for which you have an interest (referred to as non-arm's length) in the property (e.g., your own mortgage or that of a relative), the mortgage must be insured, either through CMHC or Genworth, and be administered by an approved lender. The mortgage must also be on market terms.

By holding your own mortgage in your RRSP, you can access the assets that have accumulated in your plan over the years. Many people find that placing a tangible asset, such as the mortgage on their home in their RRSP, provides a real sense of security.

> If you have a mortgage and invest in RRSPs, you probably have noticed that the rate of interest you pay on the mortgage is often greater than the rate of interest that you are paid on your RRSP, assuming that you have a guaranteed interest rate RRSP. This is because all lenders have a "spread," which is the difference between what's charged in interest on a mortgage, and what is paid in interest on deposit investments.

How to Invest in Your Own Mortgage

Here is how the plan works if you decide to invest your RRSP in your own mortgage. Let's say that you want to obtain a $100,000 mortgage and you contribute approximately $10,000 each year into your RRSP. If you deal with a lender who offers this option, you would take out the mortgage with that lender and each time you make your RRSP contribution, the lender will use these funds to purchase $10,000 of your mortgage. When you make your monthly mortgage payments, then, part of the interest you are paying on your mortgage will go into your RRSP and part to the lender. The next time you make a contribution to your RRSP, more of your mortgage will be purchased by your RRSP. Eventually, it is possible that your entire mortgage will be owned by your RRSP. From that point on, you would be making payments directly to your RRSP, in other words to yourself, rather than the lender. The set-up and administrative fees that a lender charges on this plan are fairly nominal.

Depending on the interest rates, in this hypothetical example, you could own your own mortgage within seven years or less. The reason is that the interest in your RRSP is compounding tax-free every year, thereby permitting more money to be available to pay off the mortgage.

Another attractive option is to pay your RRSP payments monthly rather than in a lump sum once a year. You will earn more money because of ongoing compounding of interest every month this way.

In most cases, you can also utilize the plan just described on revenue property as well, subject to the stipulation that the mortgage be insured by CMHC and that all the other conditions of the plan are complied with.

As in any unique plan, there are advantages and limitations. It is not for everyone. Make sure you comparison shop, receive answers to all your questions, obtain detailed written information to review, and obtain professional advice from your tax accountant.

REAL ESTATE INVESTMENT TRUSTS (REIT)

REITs were introduced into Canada in 1993 as publicly traded securities. A REIT is a company that owns, and in most cases operates, income-producing real estate, ranging from apartments, retirement homes, and multi-family residences, to shopping centres, industrial buildings, and commercial office buildings.

REITs are a popular asset class, as real estate has historically delivered consistent cash flow in addition to the preservation of capital.

Another appeal of an REIT to an investor is that a REIT offers steady and tax-advantaged income. REITs are subject to market risk in that their unit prices may rise or fall for reasons that are not directly correlated with management of the business. They offer potential capital appreciation within a conservative capital structure.

If this is an investment option that interests you, check with your financial advisor.

MORTGAGE BROKERS

Mortgage brokers perform various services, including acting as an agent for people who have money to invest and wish to do so by funding new mortgages or buying an existing mortgage at a discount. Because mortgage brokers are involved in the real estate money market, they are a natural contact source to consider if you wish to invest in mortgages.

Be sure to comparison shop before you decide on a broker with whom to invest. Compare a minimum of three mortgage brokers; look for features such as personality, expertise, nature of experience, accessibility, reputation, and service.

In terms of fees, you do not normally pay the broker for finding a mortgage to buy or someone who wants a new mortgage funded. The broker receives his payment from the borrower. In addition, the borrower pays all the associated costs of obtaining a mortgage (e.g., legal, survey, appraisal, inspection) as you might pay yourself, if you obtained a mortgage from a conventional lender.

PRIVATE MORTGAGES

You may wish to invest in mortgages by buying existing mortgages at a discount or by funding new mortgages. You can do the process yourself directly by requesting referrals from those you know, such as lawyers, realtors, or mortgage brokers. You can also place classified ads in the newspaper, through the Internet, or other communication means. You should obtain advice from a real estate lawyer beforehand, and on an ongoing basis, to make sure that your interests are protected and that you are fully complying with any provincial (e.g., mortgage broker/real estate) legislation or federal (e.g., interest rate) legislation. Alternatively, you might deal through an agent, usually a mortgage broker, as just discussed. There are advantages and disadvantages, depending on your needs.

Basically, if you deal through a broker, it can be much easier from a time, resource, peace of mind, and administrative viewpoint. On the other hand, if you feel experienced or self-confident in this area, and have the time and desire, you may wish to do it yourself, with the protection of an experienced real estate lawyer assisting you in the legal documentation and security. In this latter case, you may be able to obtain an additional and higher bonus or signing fee that would otherwise be paid by the borrower to the mortgage broker.

Remember, you do not pay a fee to the mortgage broker if you use one. In all instances, the borrower pays all out-of-pocket costs that you require, such as your legal fees for preparing and registering the mortgage, appraisal, survey and inspection fees, etc.

You may want to invest in mortgages because you believe you can obtain a better return on your money than other means. The interest that you receive from the mortgage is taxable, of course. If you are operating this investment business out of your home, it is possible you could offset home-business expenses against the income.

There are many reasons why people use private rather than conventional mortgage funding:

- They cannot meet the strict lending criteria of conventional mortgage lenders, even if the property is good security and there is lots of equity.
- They are too leveraged with other property already; that is, they have too much debt.
- They have too much other debt that is not real estate related.
- They have a poor credit history.
- They may be unemployed.
- They could be recently self-employed and therefore have no track record of income or indication of viability of the business.

- Their salary may be inadequate to be qualified by a conventional lender.
- They may be facing time-pressure constraints to acquire a good real estate buy.
- There could be an element of risk associated with the property that the lender is not willing to accept.
- The property might be an apartment building, multiplex dwelling, or raw land.
- They may want terms that are unconventional and that a conventional lender cannot offer due to their policies.
- The vendor of a property provided vendor-back mortgage financing in order to effect a property sale. Now the vendor wants to discount the mortgage and sell it in order to obtain money for other needs or purposes.

There are some key points to consider when considering the option of investing in mortgages: adhere to your investment criteria and strategies, assess the quality of real estate being used as security, determine the borrower's equity in property, assess the ability of the borrower to repay the loan, determine the amount of interest and nature of mortgage terms, and then determine the overall degree of risk relative to other investment options.

TIPS ON FUNDING A NEW MORTGAGE

In terms of establishing a cautious investment strategy and lending criteria for any mortgage investment, there are some key issues to consider and procedures to follow. Here are a few of the most common considerations, particularly when funding a new mortgage.

Determine the degree of risk. You may just want to invest in first mortgages, not second or third mortgages. Remember the issue of priorities. In the event of the borrower breaching the mortgage and the property being sold, the mortgage is paid back in priority relative to its priority of date of registration. As discussed before, a first mortgage is paid back first (it was registered first), followed by the second mortgage (it was registered second), and so on. Interest is commensurate with risk, therefore each level of mortgage (1st, 2nd, 3rd, etc.) has an increasingly higher rate of interest.

You may decide to obtain a higher return by investing in a potentially higher-risk mortgage. Alternatively, you may only want to fund people who have low-ratio financing; that is, they only have a first mortgage and will not be obtaining a second or third mortgage.

- It is essential to obtain competent professional advice from a real estate lawyer and tax accountant in advance of any deal being signed and sealed.
- Consider the benefits of using a mortgage broker.
- Ensure an appraisal of the property is done by an appraiser of your choice. You can request a conservative appraisal.
- Get a survey plan and make sure the property complies with all municipal bylaws.
- Have the building inspected by a professional inspector of your choice.
- Determine what type of property you want to fund or buy a mortgage on; for example, a house, condominium, recreational property, raw land, multi-unit dwelling, or apartment building.
- Determine the quality of real estate being used as security. For example, the quality of construction, nature of zoning, and whether it is income-producing or not. If not, there are

more risks in terms of debt-servicing capacity, hence a higher rate of interest is charged.

- Assess the location of property. The better the location, the higher the resale demand and therefore the lower the risk.

- Determine why the person really wants private new mortgage funding or wants to sell an existing private mortgage. Is that person in serious financial difficulty? Always have a credit check done.

- Determine how stringent your mortgage security requirements are. For example, let's say you are funding a mortgage on a property for an investor (e.g., a second or third mortgage). The investor owns various properties. You may wish to require that the mortgage therefore be a "blanket" mortgage. This means it is filed against the principal property being funded, as well as against several other properties owned by the investor. This would, of course, reduce your risk. Naturally, it would increase the expense to the borrower, in terms of additional legal and filing fees.

- Assess the borrower's equity in the property. You may want to have a restriction in the mortgage that no additional financing on the property can be obtained and filed without your advance written consent. Alternatively, if you didn't give your consent, any financing filed would automatically trigger the need for immediate payment on your mortgage.

- Determine the ability of the borrower to repay the loan. Utilize the various GDS and TDS ratios as a basic guideline. You may have a policy of requiring a co-signor or guarantor of the borrower's mortgage to reduce the potential risk. Do credit checks of them through your lawyer, mortgage broker, or bank.

- Determine the amount of interest that you want as a return on your investment. Your rate would normally be higher than "market" rate for your type of mortgage and degree of risk, perhaps considerably higher, depending on the circumstances and your policy. Because your mortgage is a private mortgage, the inference is that the borrower could not get funding elsewhere, hence your leverage in requesting a higher interest return and stringent conditions.

- Consider the issue of insurance thoroughly, in terms of what you require to be covered by the borrower—your lawyer can advise you. The borrower would pay all premiums. This could include life insurance on the borrower to cover the amount of the mortgage with yourself as beneficiary; mortgage insurance on the mortgage through Genworth, to protect you in case of default by the borrower, resulting in a sale of the property and subsequent shortfall to pay out your mortgage; and property insurance for fire damage and third-party liability, in the event of loss or destruction of the building, or litigation against the owner due to injury to someone on the property. You would show up on the policy as being paid first, second, or third by the insurance company, depending on the ranking of your mortgage.
- Inspect the property thoroughly yourself to get your own impressions, quite apart from having a building inspector do so on your behalf.
- Determine the geographic area within which you are prepared to invest (e.g., geographic areas that you can drive within three hours, or limited to certain areas in certain municipalities, etc.).
- Check with the municipal building department to satisfy yourself there are no outstanding work orders.
- Have your lawyer do a search on the property to determine what, if any, non-financial encumbrances there are related

to the property, for example, easements, rights-of-way, or other restrictions.

- Have a credit check done of the prospective borrower to assess his or her past credit history, payment patterns, and other matters. The borrower would have to complete a credit application authorizing you to do so. If you are using a mortgage broker, he or she would have to fill out an application. If you were doing it yourself, your lawyer could assist you in preparing an application. In the latter circumstance, you would want to become a member of your local credit bureau so that you could perform searches yourself, or alternatively have your lawyer do so and give you a copy to review. Check in the Appendix under Helpful Websites for the website address for Equifax, a credit-reporting agency.

- If the borrower is using your funds to buy a revenue property, request an "assignment of rents" document. This means that in the event the borrower defaults, you would be entitled to have the tenants pay the rent to you directly.

- Consider having an acceleration clause in the mortgage in the event the borrower defaults. That way you could demand the full amount of the mortgage be paid (accelerate the debt) rather than just the arrears. In some provinces, there are restrictions on the use of acceleration clauses.

- Consider having a prepayment penalty for closed mortgages in order to deter short-term payoffs.

- Consider a shorter-term mortgage if interest rates are rising, and a longer term mortgage if interest rates are falling. Private mortgages tend to be shorter term; for example, one year. That way money can be worked more frequently, thereby making more money. This is because each time money is advanced, there is normally a premium charged up-front, referred to as a bonus. In addition, short-term use of funds makes the money more sensitive to changing interest rates and reduces risk.

- Consider charging a bonus to grant the mortgage. A bonus is related to various factors that you would establish, such as credit rating of the borrower, whether the borrower is self-employed or employed and for how long, whether the borrower has past experience and a track record of investing in real estate, length of time the funds are being borrowed, etc. For example, you might charge a bonus of 1% to 5% of the mortgage amount being requested, in addition to the borrower covering you for all your required expenses, in addition to an above market interest rate in the mortgage. It all depends on your investment criteria and policy. Needless to say, you want to obtain expert tax and legal advice on your lending options and protections.

- Insert a clause in the mortgage that it can only be assumed by a future purchaser of the borrower's property with your prior consent. This allows you an opportunity to assess the credit-worthiness of the person who is going to assume the mortgage. Alternatively, you may want to have a clause that states that the mortgage cannot be assumed. It would have to be paid out with a penalty in the event the borrower sold the underlying property.

- Consider having the interest on the mortgage funds you advance calculated monthly rather than semi-annually. This will increase the effective rate of interest you receive, and therefore your yield; that is, the percentage return on your investment.

- Obtain a computerized printout of the mortgage interest you are going to receive so that you can calculate precisely the return that you are getting. You can obtain this printout from your accountant, mortgage broker, financial planner, conventional lender, realtor, or online. You can get excellent software programs that will assist you.

• If you want to further minimize the potential risk in a given situation, you may require that the first year's interest be prepaid. For example, if you calculate that the first year's interest on a one-year mortgage of $90,000 is $10,000, you might require that the face amount of the mortgage shows as $100,000. You only advance $90,000 to the borrower. The remaining $10,000 of that you keep for prepayment of the first year's interest. It would state this in the mortgage document, so the borrower would only need to eventually pay out the $90,000 amount of principal. This is sometimes referred to as an "impound mortgage"; in other words, the interest is impounded. There are several variants of this concept.

If you are being asked to lend money to a friend or relative, always secure your money by means of a mortgage as a condition of the loan. Whether you charge interest or not, require regular payments or not, or simply have a collateral mortgage to secure a demand promissory note, are all judgment calls, based on all the facts and circumstances. Every situation is different. The key point is to secure your money. Nothing causes more traumatic feelings and friction within the family unit or among friends than money that is not paid when expected (or not paid at all). The benefits of mortgage protection, regardless of the flexibility of the terms, far outweigh the concern you might have about being perceived as too "businesslike" or "implying a lack of trust."

If you have difficulty with this type of situation, get legal and tax advice and then attribute your decision to the advice you received. It is always more comfortable "blaming" a professional and credible "third party" for getting around awkward situations and justifying your actions! This advice is particularly important if you are lending money to a child who is married or getting married. Otherwise, if the marriage dissolves, the proceeds from the sale of the family home could be split between the spouses, unless you were originally secured by a mortgage.

If you lend money to a child or relative or friend in a business, the business could fail and the owners of the business could be held personally liable by the creditors. Judgments could be filed against the personal home and the house sold. If your funds were secured by a mortgage at the outset, you would be protected.

Tips on Buying an Existing Mortgage

The cautions outlined in the previous section also apply here if you are considering the purchase of existing mortgages. When doing so, you buy them at a discounted rate, depending on what yield or return you want to receive on your money. In legal terms, normally the mortgage is assigned to you and the original lender is notified and any consents obtained. Any associated costs are normally borne by the person selling the mortgage. The benefits of discounting are:

- You receive additional interest on your money because you are receiving interest on the amount of the discount immediately. For example, if you pay $30,000 for a $45,000 mortgage, you are receiving interest on the $15,000 discount amount. This is assuming you already have the money sitting in a term deposit, GIC, etc. You are also making money on the interest on the full $45,000.
- You receive additional money because your discount calculations are based on the current outstanding principal balance

of the mortgage, and not on a reducing principal balance which occurs as the loan payments progress. The amount of principal reduction on mortgages in the first three years is fairly minimal anyway. Most of the payments go towards interest. It is a quantifiable financial advantage to you, though.

• You have the opportunity to refinance the mortgage with the original lender before the end of the term, but only for the duration of the term, if the interest rates fall below that of the original mortgage. You would only want to do this if you are still financially ahead after taking into account any pre-payment penalties. There are several other creative options available to increase your return on your original investment.

There is a "rule of thumb" for quick calculation of the discount amount. For example, if the rate of interest on an existing second mortgage is 10%, and you wish to have the mortgage produce a return of 15%, the 5% difference is multiplied by the number of years remaining in the mortgage term (e.g., maturity date) when the principal balance is due and payable. The outcome of the calculation will be the discount, which is subtracted from the mortgage amount to determine the purchase price. This is just a guideline. You will want to obtain a computerized spreadsheet of the precise amount.

ALWAYS GET PROFESSIONAL ADVICE

The above suggestions and tips are intended to raise your awareness and street-smarts and stimulate ideas on the business of making money in mortgages. Now that you have a better understanding of the nature of investing in mortgages, you can see why having a real estate lawyer to protect your interests is so critical. You can also see why having a tax accountant to advise you is so essential to maximizing your net profit and minimizing your taxable income.

CHECKLIST 1: PREPARING FOR A MORTGAGE

As you think about taking out a mortgage, use the following questions for perspective:

1. Is your income secure?
2. Will your income increase or decrease in the future?
3. Are you planning on increasing the size of your family (e.g., children, relatives) and therefore your living expenses?
4. Will you be able to put aside a financial buffer for unexpected expenses or emergencies?
5. Are you planning to purchase the property with someone else?
6. If the answer is yes to the above question, will you be able to depend on your partner's financial contribution without interruption?
7. If you are relying on income from renting out all or part of your purchase, do you know:
   - If city bylaws permit it?
   - If the condominium corporation bylaws permit it, if you are buying a condo?

- If the mortgage company policies permit it?
- If the high-ratio mortgage insurance company permits it?

8. Have you thoroughly compared mortgage rates and features so that you know what type of mortgage and mortgage company you want to deal with?

9. Have you determined the amount of mortgage that you would be eligible for?

10. Have you considered the benefits of a pre-approved mortgage?

11. Have you considered talking to a mortgage broker?

12. Have you considered assuming an existing mortgage?

13. Have you considered the benefits of a portable mortgage?

14. Have you considered having the vendor give you a mortgage?

15. Have you determined all the expenses you will incur relating to the purchase transaction?

16. Have you completed your present and projected financial needs analysis (income and expenses)? (See Sample Form #1.)

17. Have you completed the mortgage application form, including net worth statement (assets and liabilities)? (See Sample Form #2.)

Research on the Internet

18. Have you researched mortgage brokers on the Internet?

19. Have you researched mortgage companies on the Internet?

20. Have you completed mortgage calculators on the Internet to determine your options and get a financial reality check?

21. Have you researched articles on mortgages on the Internet? (Refer to "Helpful Websites" in the Appendix.)

Questions for the mortgage broker or lender:

Interest Rates

22. What is the current interest rate?
23. How frequently is the interest calculated (semi-annually, monthly, etc.)?
24. What is the effective interest rate on an annual basis?
25. How long will the lender guarantee a pre-approved interest rate?
26. Will the lender put the guarantee in writing?
27. Will you receive a lower rate of interest if the rates fall before you finalize your mortgage?
28. Will the lender put the above reduction assurance in writing?
29. Will the lender show you the total amount of interest you will have to pay over the lifetime of the mortgage?

Amortization

30. What options do you have for amortization periods (10, 15, 20, 25, 30 years, etc.)?
31. Will the lender provide you with an amortization schedule for your loan showing your monthly payments apportioned into principal and interest?
32. Have you calculated what your monthly payments will be, based on each amortization rate?
33. Are you required to maintain the amortized monthly payment schedule if annual pre-payments are made, or will they be adjusted accordingly?

Term of the Mortgage

34. What different terms are available (6 months, 1, 2, 3, 5 years, etc.)?

35. What are the different interest rates available relating to the different terms?
36. What is the best term for your personal circumstances?

Payments

37. What will be the amount of your monthly payments based on the amortization period?
38. Are you permitted to increase the amount of your monthly payments, if you want to, without penalty?
39. Does the lender have a range of payment periods available, such as weekly, bi-weekly, monthly, etc.?
40. What is the best payment period in your personal circumstances?

Prepayment

41. What are your prepayment privileges?
    • Completely open?
    • Open with a fixed penalty or notice requirement?
    • Limited open with no penalty or notice requirement?
    • Limited open with fixed penalty or notice requirement?
    • Completely closed?
    • Some combination of the above?
42. What amount can be prepaid and what is the penalty or notice required, if applicable?
43. How long does the privilege apply in each of the above categories, if applicable?
44. When does the prepayment privilege commence (6 months, 1 year, etc.)?
45. Is there a minimum amount that has to be prepaid?
46. What form does your prepayment privilege take: an increase in payments or lump sum?

47. Is your prepayment privilege accumulative (e.g., make last year's lump sum prepayment next year)?

Taxes
48. How much are the property taxes?
49. Does the lender require a property tax payment monthly (based on projected annual tax), or is it optional?
50. Does the lender pay interest on the property tax account? If yes, what is the interest rate?

Mortgage Transaction Fees and Expenses
51. What is the appraisal fee? Is an appraisal necessary?
52. What is the survey fee? Is a survey necessary?
53. Will you be able to select a lawyer of your choice to do the mortgage work?
54. Does the lender charge a processing or administrative fee?
55. Does the lender arrange for a lawyer to do the mortgage documentation work at a flat fee, regardless of the amount of the mortgage?
56. Do you know what the out-of-pocket disbursements for the mortgage transaction will be?
57. Does the mortgage have a renewal administration fee? How much is it?

Mortgage Assumption Privileges
58. Can the mortgage be assumed if the property is sold?
59. Is the mortgage assumable with or without the lender's approval?
60. What are the assumption administrative fees, if any?
61. Will the lender release the vendor of all personal obligations under the terms of the mortgage if it is assumed?

Portability

62. Is the mortgage portable; i.e., can you transfer it to another property that you may buy? Within what timeframe do you need to buy a new property in order to keep the "old" mortgage rate and terms?

CHECKLIST 2: PURCHASE EXPENSES CHECKLIST

In addition to the actual purchase price of your investment, there are a number of other expenses to be paid on or prior to closing. Not all of these expenses will be applicable. Some provinces may have additional expenses.

Type of expense	When paid	Estimated amount
Deposits	At time of offer	_____
Mortgage application fee	At time of application	_____
Property appraisal	At time of mortgage application	_____
Property inspection	At inspection	_____
Balance of purchase price	On closing	_____
Legal fees re property transfer	On closing	_____
Legal fees re mortgage preparation	On closing	_____
Legal disbursements re property transfer	On closing	_____
Legal disbursements re mortgage preparation	On closing	_____
Mortgage broker commission	On closing	_____
Property survey	On closing	_____
Property tax holdback (by mortgage company)	On closing	_____
Land transfer or deed tax (provincial)	On closing	_____
Property purchase tax (provincial)	On closing	_____
Property tax adjustment (local/municipal)	On closing	_____
Goods and services tax (GST) (federal)	On closing	_____
New Home Warranty Program fee	On closing	_____
Mortgage interest adjustment (by mortgage company)	On closing	_____
Sales tax on chattels purchased from vendor (provincial)	On closing	_____

Type of expense	When paid	Estimated amount
Adjustments for fuel, taxes, etc.	On closing	_____
Mortgage lender insurance premium (CMHC or Genworth)	On closing	_____
Condominium maintenance fee adjustment	On closing	_____
Home and property insurance	On closing	_____
Life insurance premium on amount of outstanding mortgage	On closing	_____
Moving expenses	At time of move	_____
Utility connection charges	At time of move	_____
Redecorating and refurbishing costs	Shortly after purchase	_____
Immediate repair and maintenance costs	Shortly after purchase	_____
House and garden implements	Shortly after purchase	_____
Other expenses (list):		
_____	_____	_____
_____	_____	_____
_____	_____	_____
TOTAL CASH REQUIRED		$_____

SAMPLE FORM #1
Personal Cost-of-Living Budget (Monthly)

I. Income (Average monthly income, actual or estimated)

Salary, bonuses, and commissions	$ _____
Dividends	$ _____
Interest income	$ _____
Pension income	$ _____
Other:	$ _____
	$ _____
TOTAL MONTHLY INCOME (A)	$ _____

II. Expenses

Regular Monthly Payments:

Rent or mortgage payments	$ _____
Automobile(s)	$ _____
Appliances/TV/Cable	$ _____
Internet charges	$ _____
Home improvement loan	$ _____
Credit card payments (not covered elsewhere)	$ _____
Personal loan	$ _____
Medical plan	$ _____
Instalment and other loans	$ _____
Life insurance premiums	$ _____
House insurance	$ _____
Other insurance premiums (auto, extended medical, etc.)	$ _____
RRSP deductions	$ _____
Pension fund (employer)	$ _____
Investment plan(s)	$ _____
Miscellaneous	$ _____

Other: $ _____
                                                    $ _____

**TOTAL REGULAR MONTHLY
PAYMENTS** $ _____

Household Operating Expenses:
  Telephone $ _____
  Gas and electricity $ _____
  Heat $ _____
  Water and garbage $ _____
  Other household expenses
  (repairs, maintenance, etc.) $ _____
  Other: $ _____
                                                    $ _____

**TOTAL HOUSEHOLD OPERATING
EXPENSES** $ _____

Food Expenses:
  At home $ _____
  Away from home $ _____
  TOTAL FOOD EXPENSES $ _____

Personal Expenses:
  Clothing, dry cleaning, laundry $ _____
  Drugs $ _____
  Transportation (other than auto) $ _____
  Medical/dental $ _____
  Daycare $ _____
  Education (self) $ _____
  Education (children) $ _____
  Membership dues $ _____

Gifts and donations $ _____
Travel $ _____
Recreation $ _____
Newspapers, magazines, books $ _____
Automobile maintenance, gas, parking $ _____
Spending money, allowances $ _____
Other: $ _____
     $ _____
TOTAL PERSONAL EXPENSES $ _____

Tax Expenses:
Federal and provincial income taxes $ _____
Home property taxes $ _____
Other: $ _____
     $ _____
TOTAL TAX EXPENSES $ _____

III. Summary of Expenses

Regular monthly payments $ _____
Household operating expenses $ _____
Food expenses $ _____
Personal expenses $ _____
Tax expenses $ _____
TOTAL MONTHLY EXPENSES   (B) $ _____

TOTAL MONTHLY DISPOSABLE
INCOME AVAILABLE   (A − B) $ _____
(Subtract total monthly expenses from total monthly income.)

SAMPLE FORM #2

Personal Net Worth Statement

(This type of information is commonly requested by lenders.)

Name _____

Date of birth___/___/___

Social insurance number _____

Street address_____

City / Province / Postal code _____

_____

Home phone _____

Business _____

How long at address? _____ Years _____Months

__Own __Rent __Other

Occupation _____

Company _____

How long with employer? _____Years _____Months

Employer's phone _____

___Married ___Not married ___Separated ___Divorced

Number of dependants _____

Your principal financial institution and address

_____

_____

Personal Data on Your Spouse

Under the laws of Canada and of some provinces, your spouse may have a legal interest or obligation arising from your business dealings and may also have an interest in your personal assets.

Spouse's name _____

Spouse's occupation _____

Spouse currently employed by _____

Spouse's work phone _____

How long with employer? _____Years _____Months

Financial Information

As at _____ day of _____month, 20__

Assets (list and describe all assets)   Value

Total of chequing accounts $ _____

Total of savings accounts $ _____

Life insurance cash surrender value $ _____

Automobile: Make _____ Year _____ $ _____

Stocks and bonds (see Schedule A attached) $ _____

Accounts/notes receivable (please itemize):

_____ $ _____

_____ $ _____

_____ $ _____

Term deposits (cashable) $ _____

Real estate (see Schedule B attached) $ _____

Retirement plans:

  RRSP $ _____

  Employment pension plan $ _____

  Other $ _____

Other assets (household goods, etc.)

  Art $ _____

  Jewellery $ _____

  Antiques $ _____

  Other $ _____

TOTAL ASSETS   (A) $ _____

Liabilities

(List credit cards, open lines of credit, and other liabilities including alimony and child support.)

	Balance Owing	Monthly Payment
Bank loans	$ _____	$ _____
Mortgages on real estate owned (see Schedule B attached)	$ _____	$ _____
Monthly rent payment	$ _____	$ _____
Credit cards (please itemize):		
_____	$ _____	$ _____
_____	$ _____	$ _____
_____	$ _____	$ _____
_____	$ _____	$ _____
Money borrowed from life insurance policy	$ _____	$ _____
Margin accounts	$ _____	$ _____
Current income tax owing	$ _____	$ _____
Other obligations (please itemize):		
_____	$ _____	$ _____
_____	$ _____	$ _____
_____	$ _____	$ _____
TOTAL MONTHLY PAYMENTS		$ _____

TOTAL LIABILITIES (B) $ _____

NET WORTH (A – B) $ _____

Income Sources

Income from alimony, child support, or separate maintenance does not have to be stated unless you want it considered.

Your gross monthly salary $ _____

Your spouse's gross monthly salary $ _____

Net monthly rental (from Schedule B attached) $ _____

Other income (please itemize):

_____ $ _____

_____ $ _____

_____ $ _____

TOTAL $ _____

Sundry Personal Obligations

Please provide details below if you answer yes to the following question:

Are you providing your personal support for obligations not listed above (i.e., co-signer, endorser, guarantor)?

____ Yes ____ No

Details of any of the above:_____

_____

Schedule A: Stocks, Bonds, and Other Investments

Quantity	Description	Where Quoted	Market Value	Pledged as collateral	
				Yes	No

TOTAL _____

Schedule B: Real Estate Owned

Please provide information on your share only of real estate owned.

Property address (primary residence):_____

Legal description:_____

Street _____

City _____ Province _____

Type of property _____

Present market value: $ _____

Amount of mortgage liens: 1st $ _____ 2nd $ _____

Gross monthly income rental _____

Monthly mortgage payments: 1st $_____ 2nd $_____

Monthly taxes, insurance, maintenance,
and miscellaneous: _____

Net monthly rental income $_____ $_____

Name of mortgage holder(s):

First mortgage _____

Second mortgage _____

Percentage ownership: _____% Month/year acquired: _____

Purchase price $_____

General Information

Please provide details if you answer yes to any of the following questions:

Have you ever had an asset repossessed?	Yes ____	No ____
Are you party to any claims or lawsuits?	Yes ____	No ____
Have you ever declared bankruptcy?	Yes ____	No ____
Do you owe any taxes prior to the current year?	Yes ____	No ____

Details:

_____

_____

_____

_____

_____

_____

_____

_____

_____

The undersigned declare(s) that the statements made herein are for the purpose of obtaining business financing and are to the best of my/our knowledge true and correct. The applicant(s) consent(s) to the Bank making any enquiries it deems necessary to reach a decision on this application, and consent(s) to the disclosure at any time of any credit information about me/us to any credit reporting agency or to anyone with whom I/we have financial relations.

Date:_____

Signature of applicant(s) above _____

SAMPLE FORM #3
Calculating Your Gross Debt-Service (GDS) Ratio

Your GDS ratio is calculated by adding your monthly mortgage principal, interest, and taxes (PIT) together and dividing that figure by your monthly income. Guidelines have been set that generally allow a maximum of 27% to 30% or more of your gross income, depending on the financial institution, to be used for the mortgage PIT.

$$\text{GDS ratio} = \frac{\textbf{Monthly principal + Interest + Taxes (PIT)}}{\textbf{Monthly income}}$$

Gross (pre-tax) *monthly* income of purchaser(s) $ _____
Other forms of income (e.g., annual),
averaged to monthly $ _____
TOTAL MONTHLY INCOME $ _____

Estimate monthly property tax on home
(net after any provincial homeowners' grant is taken
into consideration, if applicable) $ _____

1. To estimate the *maximum* monthly mortgage payment plus property taxes you could carry (monthly PIT), calculate 30% of the total monthly income:
30% of $ _____ $ _____

2. To estimate the *maximum* monthly mortgage payment, not including taxes (PI), that you could carry, subtract the monthly tax amount from the monthly PIT:

Monthly PIT	$ _____
Less: Monthly property tax	$ _____
MAXIMUM MONTHLY MORTGAGE PAYMENT	$ _____
(not including taxes) = Monthly PI	

Maximum mortgage available under GDS ratio
guidelines $ _____

SAMPLE FORM #4:
Calculating Your Total Debt-Service (TDS) Ratio

Most lenders require that an applicant meet a TDS ratio, in addition to looking at the GDS ratio. The TDS ratio is generally a maximum of 35% to 40% or more of gross income—actual rules may vary between financial institutions. The TDS ratio is calculated in much the same way as the GDS ratio, but takes into consideration all other debts and loans you may have.

$$\text{TDS ratio} = \frac{\text{Monthly Principal} + \text{Interest} + \text{Taxes (PIT)} + \text{Other monthly payments}}{\text{Monthly Income}}$$

Gross (pre-tax) monthly income of
purchaser(s) $_____
Other forms of income (e.g., annual) averaged
to monthly $_____
TOTAL MONTHLY INCOME $_____

Other monthly payments:
   Credit cards $_____
   Other mortgages $_____
   Car loan $_____
   Other loans $_____
   Alimony/child support $_____
   Charge accounts $_____

Other debts (list): $_____

_____ $_____

_____ $_____

_____ $_____

TOTAL OTHER MONTHLY PAYMENTS $_____

To calculate your TDS ratio, take 40% of $ _____ (total monthly income) = $ _____ available for monthly principal + interest + taxes + other payments (PIT + Other).

To estimate the *maximum monthly mortgage payment* you could carry within your allowable TDS ratio:

Monthly PIT + Other $ _____
Less: Other monthly payments $ _____
SUBTOTAL $ _____

Less: Estimated property taxes $ _____
MAXIMUM MONTHLY
MORTGAGE PAYMENT $ _____

Maximum mortgage available under
TDS Ratio guidelines $ _____

HELPFUL WEBSITES

Here are some websites to assist you in your information and contacts research before buying a home or obtaining a mortgage or other forms of financing.

General Information

Google Internet Search	www.google.ca
National Real Estate Institute Inc.	www.homebuyer.ca
Canadian Estate Planning Institute Inc.	www.estateplanning.ca
Canadian Enterprise Development Group Inc.	www.smallbiz.ca

Mortgage Information and Calculators

Canadian Mortgage and Housing Corporation	www.cmhc.ca
Canadian Institute of Mortgage Brokers and Lenders	www.cimbl.ca

Mortgage Insurance and Credit Reports

Canadian Mortgage and Housing Corporation	www.cmhc.ca
Genworth Financial Canada	www.genworth.ca
Equifax Canada	www.equifax.ca

Real Estate Listings

Multiple Listing Service	www.mls.ca

Housing Surveys and Stats

Royal LePage Survey of Canadian House Prices	www.royallepage.ca
Canadian Mortgage and Housing Corporation	www.cmhc.ca

Professional Associations

Appraisal Institute of Canada	www.aicanada.ca
Canadian Association of Home and Property Inspectors	www.cahpi.ca
Canadian Home Builders' Association	www.chbi.ca
The Royal Architectural Institute of Canada	www.raic.org
Canadian Bar Association	www.cba.org
Canadian Institute of Chartered Accountants	www.cica.ca
Certified General Accountants Association of Canada	www.cga-canada.org
Canadian Institute of Mortgage Brokers and Lenders	www.cimbl.ca
Canadian Real Estate Association	www.crea.ca
Financial Advisors Association of Canada	www.advocis.ca
Financial Planners Standards Council of Canada	www.cfp-ca.org
Insurance Brokers Association of Canada	www.ibac.ca
Canadian Life and Health Insurance Association	www.clhia.ca

Federal Government

Canadian Mortgage and Housing Corporation	www.cmhc.ca
Statistics Canada	www.statcan.ca
Bank of Canada	www.bankofcanada.ca
Canada Revenue Agency	www.cra-arc.gc.ca

Glossary

Amortization period: The actual number of years it will take to repay a mortgage loan in full. This can be well in excess of the loan's term. For example, mortgages often have five-year terms but 25-year amortization periods.

Appraised value: An estimate of the value of the property offered as security for a mortgage loan. This appraisal is done for mortgage lending purposes, and may not reflect the market value of the property.

Assumption agreement: A legal document signed by a home buyer, which requires the buyer to assume responsibility for the obligations of a mortgage made by a former owner.

Blended payments: Equal payments consisting of both a principal and an interest component, paid each month during the term of the mortgage. The principal portion increases each month, while the interest portion decreases; but the total monthly payment does not change.

Canada Mortgage and Housing Corporation (CMHC): The federal Crown corporation which administers the National Housing Act. CMHC services include providing housing information and assistance, financing, and insuring high-ratio home purchase loans for lenders.

Charge: A document registered against a property, stating that someone has or believes he or she has a claim on the property, e.g., a mortgage.

Closing: The actual completion of the transaction acknowledging satisfaction of all legal and financial obligations between buyer and seller, and acknowledging the deed or transfer of title and disbursement of funds to appropriate parties.

Closing costs: The expenses over and above the purchase price of buying and selling real estate.

Closing date: The date on which the sale of a property becomes final and the new owner takes possession.

CMHC: *(See Canada Mortgage and Housing Corporation.)*

Collateral mortgage: A loan backed up by a promissory note and the security of a mortgage on a property. The money borrowed may be used for the purchase of the property itself or for another purpose, such as home renovations or a vacation.

Conventional mortgage: A mortgage loan which does not exceed 75% of the appraised value or of the purchase price of the property, whichever is the lesser. Mortgages that exceed this limit must be insured by mortgage insurance, such as that provided by CMHC and Genworth Canada Financial. (See *Fixed-rate mortgage.*)

Conveyancing: The transfer of property, or title to property, from one party to another.

Deed: This document conveys the title of the property to the purchaser. Different terminology may be used in different provincial jurisdictions.

Down payment: An initial amount of money (in the form of cash) put forward by the purchaser. Usually it represents the difference between the purchase price and the amount of the mortgage loan.

Encumbrance: (See *Charge.*)

Equity: The difference between the price for which a property could be sold and the total debts registered against it.

Escrow: The holding of a deed or contract by a third party until fulfillment of certain stipulated conditions between the contracting parties.

Estate: The title or interest one has in property such as real estate and personal property that can, if desired, be passed on to survivors at the time of one's death.

Fee simple: A manner of owning land in one's own name and free of any conditions, limitations, or restrictions.

Fixed-rate mortgage: This is the conventional mortgage that normally has a term of from one to 10 years, and amortized over 20–30 years.

Floating-rate mortgage: Another term for *Variable-rate mortgage*.

Foreclosure: A legal procedure whereby the lender obtains ownership of the property following default by the borrower on the mortgage.

Genworth: Genworth Financial Canada is the largest private insurer of high-ratio mortgages in Canada.

High-ratio mortgage: A conventional mortgage loan which exceeds 75% of the appraised value or purchase price of the property. Such a mortgage must be insured by either CMHC or Genworth Financial Canada (Genworth).

Mortgagee: The lender.

Mortgagor: The borrower.

National Housing Act (NHA) Loan: A mortgage loan which is insured by CMHC to certain maximums.

Offer to purchase: The document which sets forth all the terms and conditions under which a purchaser offers to purchase his unit. This offer, when accepted by the seller, becomes a binding agreement of purchase and sale.

PI: Principal and interest due on a mortgage.

PIT: Principal, interest, and taxes due on a mortgage.

Principal: The amount you actually borrowed, or the portion of it still owing on the original loan.

Purchase and sale agreement: (See *Agreement of purchase and sale.*)

Rescission: That period of time following the sale during which the buyer can change his mind, cancel the purchase agreement, and get a refund of funds paid on deposit. It varies from province to province from approximately three to 30 days.

Title: Generally, the evidence of right which a person has to the possession of property.

Variable Rate Mortgage: The mortgage rate varies with the prime rate fixed by the mortgage company, which is based on the prime rate of interest set by the Bank of Canada weekly. Generally, it is one or more percentage points lower than the conventional fixed-rate mortgage.

Vendor: A person selling a piece of property.

Vendor take-back: A procedure wherein the setter (vendor) of a property provides some or all of the mortgage financing in order to sell the property. Also referred to as *vendor financing.*

Index

Reader Feedback and Educational Resources

Your candid feedback and constructive suggestions for improvement of future editions of this book would be most welcome. Feedback can be submitted through the website listed below.

Please also refer to this website if you would like further educational information, and to find out how you can be put on a mailing list for a free e-mail newsletter or be kept informed about any upcoming seminars in your area relating to real estate in Canada.

www.homebuyer.ca

About the Author

Douglas Gray, B.A., LL.B., formerly a practising real estate and business lawyer, has extensive experience in all aspects of real estate and mortgage financing. He has acted on behalf of buyers, sellers, developers, investors, lenders, borrowers, tenants, and landlords. He also has wide experience as a personal investor in real estate for over 35 years, as well as being a landlord of various properties.

Doug morphed from a legal career to being a consultant, columnist, speaker, and author of 22 best-selling books, some of which are published in up to nine foreign language editions. The topics of his books cover small business, personal finance, retirement and estate planning. He has also written seven books on real estate, including his two most recent releases published by John Wiley & Sons Canada, Ltd: *Making Money in Real Estate: The Canadian Guide to Profitable Investment in Residential Real Estate*, Revised Edition, and *101 Streetsmart Condo Buying Tips for Canadians*.

Doug lives in Vancouver, B.C.

His website is: www.homebuyer.ca